From the best selling author of "The Order of Melchizedek!"

the CONSCIOUSNESS *of* NOW

NEW ORDER OF WISDOM

...Living a Spirit controlled STRESS-FREE-LIFE in a Chaotic World!

By Dr. Francis Myles

Published by

Order of Melchizedek Holdings LLC (in partnership with)
The Order of Leadership University AKA OMLU/NIC
P.O. Box 122242
Arlington, TX 76012

For Worldwide Distribution
Printed in the United States

ISBN :9780615947303

ACKNOWLEDGMENTS

WHAT WE BECOME IN GOD is a sum total of the divine encounters we have had, the people we have met, our experiences, and the books we have read. The saying "No man is an island" is certainly true in the context of authoring this book. I want to acknowledge the impact that the following men and women of God have had on my life: Dr. Jonathan David (my father in the faith), Apostle Harrison Chileshe (my pastor), Apostle John Eckhardt (who introduced me to the apostolic), Dr. John P. Kelly (who commissioned me as an apostle), Dr Tim Johns, Apostle Robert Ricciardelli, Prophet Kevin Leal (my big brother), Dr. G.E. Bradshaw (my covenant brother and spiritual covering), Danny Seay (who has become a living example of this book's message), Bishop Robert Smith (who introduced me to the message on the One New Man), Apostle Cheryl Fortson—their teachings and personal conversations with me over the years have added to the richness of this book.

While the material in this book is original, there are a few quotes throughout that have been taken from the published works of other notable Christian authors, which add depth to the topic or focus. Each is documented in the Endnote section.

HALL OF APPRECIATION

"The Lord gave the word: great was the company of those that published it" (Psalm 68:11 KJV).

I T HAS BEEN SAID that great projects are never the work of one man, but the collective effort of a *team that shares a common destiny.* I want to give a heartfelt "God bless you" to the following brothers and sisters for making the publishing of this book a reality. May God give you a tremendous harvest for every person who will be transformed by the truths contained within.

Carmela Real Myles for being the love of my life and an amazing glue and connector for God's Kingdom

Linda Reiter and Becky Chaille for Editing this Manuscript

My parents, Daniel and Ester Mbepa, for raising me in the fear of the Lord

Dr. Jesse Bielby

Pastor David Brace

Linda and Raymond Vega, Stockbridge, GA

Larry Scott, Castries, St. Lucia

Danny and Diane Seay, Lenexa, Kansas

Karen Hosey, Stockbridge, GA

Kyle Newton, for helping me fine-tune this revelation

Members of Royal Priesthood Fellowship Church in Tempe, Arizona

TABLE OF CONTENTS

PREFACE

There are forces seen and unseen in the world we live in that are engaged in an ongoing and calculated assault on the subject of "Consciousness" as it relates to knowing the person of God. At the frontlines of this assault on "Consciousness" are some unsuspecting members of the New Age movement, who refer to Consciousness as an elevated sense of personal enlightenment. Unfortunately, personal enlightenment falls short of the true meaning and purpose of biblical "Consciousness." Consciousness, which does not lead us into the outstretched arms of a loving God, is no Consciousness at all, but a deceptive blanket of darkness. Personal enlightenment that falls short of revealing the true and living God who is the essence of light is simply a cunningly weaved cloak of deception. This book is designed to help you break through this proverbial veil of deceit into the glorious inheritance of the saints in Light!

*And no marvel; for Satan himself is transformed into an **angel of light***

(2 Corinthians 11:14, KJV).

"The enemy always tries to mirror everything that God is doing. In order to get a lie to be believed, it has to be very close to the truth, or close to an exact replica with a slight twist - just enough to be turned sideways. This would be considered by most as "form," but the levels of "form" can be very complicated and dual purposed. Everyone reading this has probably heard of the New Age movement. In 'Christian' terminology the New Age movement is evil and against Christ, holding many false doctrines, which 'Christians' must watch out for and never allow into their lives. There are countless of these doctrines that could be mentioned, but I will focus on only two to get the picture across."

Awakening: (Biblical counterpart = rebirth)

General world or religious view: Awakening is the increase of awareness where the person starts to see life from a new perspective: a unity of likeness and love where everything is interlinked and by doing damage to another, you are doing it to yourself. Awakening increases your level of responsibility and accountability. You, as the "New Age" movement, believe you are awakening to a higher level of purity, where you can no longer be influenced by that from which you were previously bound. You have thus stepped out of it and have become a 'new man' with new sight and desires.

Awakening that is rebirth: Rebirth is being filled with the Holy Spirit through the true acceptance of Jesus Christ as your personal savior. Blindness is removed, new sight restored and what once held you in slavery can no longer attack you, and because of being in the Spirit (staying connected to God), it can no longer influence you like it did before. In short, that which bound you previously has no more power over you, or the previous bondage is greatly diminished. Any remaining obstacles can be overcome through your rebirth and your connection to God through the power of the Holy Spirit.

The difference between the two forms is that one is self-oriented and the other works only through your connection to God. It's the same mirror image found in many aspects of distortion related to true spiritual growth. This action of connection to God is not a mindless one, as many would have you believe. It is to be a conscious transformation, as you will see in "Consciousness" below.

Consciousness: (Biblical counterpart = being spirituallyminded)

General world or religious view: *Consciousness is a form of higher awareness. One where your everyday awareness, and being conscious of that awareness, is transcended. Consciousness is also a direct result of awakening. One who has achieved consciousness or enlightenment sees the world through different "eyes." The sensory world no longer plays the major role in determining the way ahead, but a more spiritually oriented sight, which is termed "consciousness." This new awareness is said to be all the physical senses and sensory perception combined with standard awareness. Consciousness is the added extra sensory perception. It is a new form of sight or understanding.*

Consciousness that is being spiritually-minded: *Consciousness is the realization of the glory and living reality of God. God is a living God! His Holy Spirit comes to reside in you, as the Helper. Consciousness is the awareness of the daily experience and interaction of your soul/spirit with the Holy Spirit. Consciousness is also the "new" you, the "true" you as created by God originally before any structures and limits were placed in your mind. In short, you cannot be the real unadulterated "you" unless you have consciousness! It is an ever-growing principle, from milk to solids to meat to...*

Consciousness is the aspect of you that will increase and grow so that your strength and purity, with the help of God, might increase. Without consciousness, you cannot really see or obey any of the real laws that are for your protection. Many want sight and gifts, but without consciousness, they will never have true sight. God gave us a full description of true consciousness in the commandment; *"Love the Lord with your whole heart, soul, mind and all your strength."* That ability, that growing aspect in your life is called "consciousness." You should be asking yourself, "Do I really want consciousness to be stolen from me?" If, like many others, you have been programmed by society, religion, peers or any other form of 'man made instruction' of religious order, it is highly likely that you have been taught that consciousness is against God. Nothing can be further from the truth. Consciousness is what gives you true free will and this will is needed to serve the Lord properly. Do not give it up, because form has set a trap in your life. Remember when you wish to get out of it; will try to hinder you. Be as wise as serpents and as harmless as doves.

Welcome to a life driven by true biblical "Consciousness." This book will show you how "Consciousness" is the key to living a stress free life in a world driven by the engines of chaos. The most powerful form of "Consciousness" is what the Holy Spirit calls "The Consciousness of NOW." The Lord told me that this "Consciousness" realigns man's spirit, soul and body with the eternal God, while simultaneously canceling the tyranny of time continuum over man's consciousness. This book is about Kingdom secrets for living in the "NOW," and how this type of living eliminates stress and chaos from the lives of those who have developed this kind of "Consciousness." Living in the "NOW" will also exponentially increase our ability to walk intimately with the LORD!

God's Servant,

Dr. Francis Myles

Chapter One

THE WAR ON CONSCIOUSNESS

The greatest and most lethal war that the Body of Christ is involved in is the war on consciousness. *The devil is not as interested in robbing us of our financial or social status as much as he is interested in stripping us of consciousness.* This is because the demonic powers know that we cannot manifest our sonship inheritance in Christ stripped of "Consciousness." *Without consciousness we will be stripped of our connection to God and the much-needed daily interaction with the precious Holy Spirit; making a life of obedience to God impossible to sustain.* We will find ourselves grappling in the dark trying to do by the arm of the flesh what God intended to be done in the spiritual realm through the power of His Spirit. The Scriptures declare loudly, *"It is not by might nor by power but by My Spirit says the Lord of hosts!"* (Zechariah 4:6, NKJV).

1

RELATING TO CONSCIOUSNESS

Now may the God of peace make you holy in every way, and may your whole spirit and soul and body be kept blameless until our Lord Jesus Christ comes again

(1 Thessalonians 5:23).

Without a shadow of doubt, the most important spiritual battle that believers are engaged in is the "War on consciousness." The reason for this becomes obvious when we examine the above passage of Scripture. The Apostle Paul tells us that we are triune beings consisting of spirit, soul and body. *We are essentially spirit-beings, who possess a soul and live in a body.* What is of note here is that God created us to relate to consciousness on all of these three levels.

1. Man's **"spirit"** gives him or her, the ability for God-consciousness. God is a Spirit (John 4:24) and, in consequence, can only be discerned through a man's spirit. This is why the first thing that the Holy Spirit does in regeneration when a person turns to the Lord is to resurrect their spirit into a newness of life in Christ Jesus. Once a sinner's spirit is made alive unto God through the shed blood of Christ, their level of God-consciousness begins to increase almost immediately. This is because the Lord knows that no one can experience His glorious presence beyond his or her ability to relate to consciousness. Consciousness is like the "suction force" in a vacuum cleaner; without it, the vacuum has no way of relating to the dust on the carpeted floor. Running a vacuum cleaner without suction force over a dirty piece of carpet will do us no good. We will make a lot of noise and waste our energy without having cleaned the carpet.

    In like manner, without "consciousness" believers have no way of relating to the supernatural realm and the God who governs this powerful invisible world. Man's spirit not only gives him God-consciousness but it is also the vehicle that allows him to relate to the invisible world of all created spirit beings. This invisible world of created spirit beings consists of both holy and fallen angels. But without consciousness, the power and activity of these angelic beings will be lost on us. Many people fall prey to the seductive influence of evil spirits because they lack "God-Consciousness." This would explain why the writer of the book of Hebrews warned the Hebraic believers in Yeshua, to make sure that they did not "entertain angels unawares" (see Hebrews 13:1-3). Unfortunately, many people, including many members of the Body of Christ, are far more conscious of the activity and presence of demonic powers, than they are of the glory and reality of the living God. This is why the supernatural eludes so many churches in the Western world where intellect has replaced God-consciousness.

2. Man's "**soul**" gives him or her the ability for what is known as "self-consciousness." This is because man's soul consists of "will, mind and emotions." The presence of these three faculties in the soul of man makes the "soul" the true seat of self. This is why one of the quickest ways to enslave human beings and turn them into a plantation of robotic machines is to strip them of self-consciousness. Karl Marx, the founder of modern day communism, mastered the art of stripping individuals of self-consciousness and replacing it with what he called "collective consciousness." *To create collective consciousness he created the philosophy of communism where the needs of the individual are dwarfed by the needs of the State.* But collective consciousness is a demonic strategy to strip man of consciousness, by forcing him to surrender the free exercise of his God-given will, mind and emotions to the State.

Using the doctrine of "collective consciousness" a deranged maniac in the form of Adolph Hitler rose to power and drove an entire nation of free men and women into a murderous frenzy. Before this deranged maniac committed suicide, six million Jews had died in poisoned gas chambers and millions more around the world had died in two bloody world wars instigated by him. After Adolf Hitler committed suicide, the spell of "collective consciousness" that he had cast over his fellow Germans, began to fade away. In the aftermath of the carnage, most Germans were horrified at the sight of what they had done under Hitler's reign. They could not believe that one man had successfully frozen the responsible use of their will, mind and emotions. Like zombies, Hitler led many of his fellow Germans to commit the worst genocide in human history. Using the doctrine of collective consciousness, the devil systematically stripped many Germans of biblical "self-consciousness." Like robotic machines, the entire German population marched to war under Hitler's drumbeat in a demonic zombie-like fashion.

Soul-driven "self-consciousness" is what enables us to make choices for ourselves independent of the general trend of the populace. Legendary Christian writer and thinker C.S. Lewis says, *"The greatest gift that God ever gave us is the gift to be ourselves."* This is why I want to re-emphasize the fact that the most important spiritual battle that believers (Kingdom citizens) are engaged in is the *"War on Consciousness."*

Mental asylums all over the world are a bitter testament to the ferocious demonically engineered assault on consciousness. When a person becomes insane, he or she loses consciousness. The State quickly commits them to a mental institution where for the most part their life is governed exclusively by the choices of others. By this definition, the world is full of "spiritually insane people" who think that they are free but have actually given up their "consciousness" to the devil. *Demonic entities remotely control most of their choices, even though most would swear that they are in control of their choices.* But when such persons come into the saving knowledge of Jesus Christ, they suddenly realize just how much control the devil had over the consciousness. This book will teach you how to fight for "biblical consciousness," without giving up control of your life to the demonic powers.

3. Finally, man's "**physical body**" gives him or her the ability for "world consciousness." Man's physical body is the only way he can be conscious of his immediate physical surroundings. This would explain why a very loving mother in a casket remains emotionally unresponsive to the wailing of her dear children. Her death has, in this case, stripped her of all world consciousness. I have heard the stories of men and women who had amazing near-death experiences. Some have testified of the things that they saw and heard their families say and do while they were in a deep coma.

4. In the following passage of Scripture, the Apostle Paul tells us about a heavenly encounter that God gave him.

    ...I will reluctantly tell about visions and revelations from the Lord. [2] I was caught up to the third heaven fourteen years ago. Whether I was in my body or out of my body, I don't know—only God knows. [3] Yes, only God knows whether I was in my body or outside my body. But I do know [4] that I was caught up to paradise and heard things so astounding that they cannot be expressed in words, things no human is allowed to tell (2 Corinthians 12:1-4).

    In the above passage of scripture the Apostle Paul tells us about a heavenly encounter that God gave him. He was supernaturally teleported into the presence of God. He did not know whether he was in his physical body or outside the body. *The prophetic experience was most likely an out-of-body experience.* This would explain why he could not remember the participation of his body in the whole encounter . Demonic possession or oppression of the body is a demonic ploy to strip mankind of his "world consciousness."

I once prayed for a black woman in South Africa who had been insane for at least twenty years. She used to sleep in dirty tunnels and ditches. She ate from trashcans and she was scantily dressed. After I prayed for her, she was gloriously delivered. When she came back to her senses, she gasped at the scanty dressing that covered her. I immediately instructed the women in the crusade to find something for her to wear. While she was robbed of both self and world-consciousness, this woman did not care about how she looked. But after she recovered her "consciousness" she demanded an immediate change in attire. She knew immediately that she was naked and did not like it one bit.

RATIONALITY AND TANGIBILITY

Rationality and tangibility are the diseases of our modern age. How is it possible that we are so infected that we, the human race at large, have no consciousness? Could it be that we have been tricked into this tangible reality and that this trap, this "realness" we are striving for is not real?

The lack of consciousness that we are experiencing at present is our own fault. Man strives to "possess everything in sight" and no matter how many possessions he has, he is never satisfied. Our greed of conquering everything in sight does not stop at the physical; instead, all aspects of spiritual reality have to become tangible to suit our needs. We have taken the Creator and put Him in a box. The box was created so that we, with our limited capacity, could make Him tangible and rule over this aspect of divinity. We claim to have understanding, and our religious leaders claim to know where they are leading the herds and we the people follow without questioning.

This is what we call the "advance of the 21st century." In all reality we are going backwards and are slowly but surely advancing in our reconstruction of the tower of Babel. With full information overload the scientists of today and the religious leaders supposedly in opposition to each other all proclaim in unity. We say that "perception is reality" and the awareness of such is consciousness. But how many people have fallen prey to this lie? Consciousness has nothing to do with so-called reality or, in fact, our rational destructive explanation of it. The reality inferred to by rationalizing is nothing but the age-old illusion of the letter. It is the spirit that quickens and God is Spirit; those who worship Him must worship in spirit and truth. How many followers of Christ are even aware that they are trapped in a destructive cycle and are being stopped from realizing the presence and power of God? (Excerpt from www.stopfollowingman.org)

THE POWER OF CONSCIOUSNESS

Now Jacob went out from Beersheba and went toward Haran. ¹¹So he came to a certain place and stayed there all night, because the sun had set. And he took one of the stones of that place and put it at his head, and he lay down in that place to sleep. ¹²Then he dreamed, and behold, a ladder was set up on the earth, and its top reached to heaven; and there the angels of God were ascending and descending on it. ¹³And behold, the Lord stood above it and said: "I am the Lord God of Abraham your father and the God of Isaac; the land on which you lie I will give to you and your descendants. ¹⁴Also your descendants shall be as the dust of the earth; you shall spread abroad to the west and the east, to the north and the south; and in you and in your seed all the families of the earth shall be blessed. ¹⁵Behold, I am with you and will keep you wherever you go, and will bring you back to this land; for I will not leave you until I have done what I have spoken to you." ¹⁶Then Jacob awoke from his sleep and said, "Surely the Lord is in this place, and I did not know it"(Genesis 28:10-16, NKJV).

Perhaps there is no other Old Testament passage that demonstrates the incredible power of biblical "consciousness" like the above passage of Scripture. Jacob is fleeing to Syria to escape his elder brother's ploy to kill him for stealing his *firstborn birthright*. We know from Scripture that he left in a hurry to escape his brother's murderous rage. I believe he kept looking back as he made his escape to make sure he was not being followed. The consciousness of any person travelling under such circumstances is a "fear consciousness." This kind of consciousness only serves to strengthen the demonic technology against the person who is subject to it. Jacob's consciousness concerning the glory and reality of the living God was dismal at best.

By a divine confluence of paths, when Jacob stopped to rest at Bethel (Bethel is the same place where Abraham had made an altar unto the Lord God) he had walked into an open heavenly portal and did not know it! When he went to sleep, he dreamed of a ladder that reached up to the third heaven. Angels were ascending and descending on this prophetic ladder. The Lord was at the top of the ladder. He spoke to Jacob about the Abrahamic Covenant and his inherent destiny. God told him that He would give him the land he was sleeping on, just as He had promised his father, Abraham. God also showed him the "now" reality of His presence in his life. Solemnly, God told him that He would never leave nor forsake him until He fulfilled in his life everything He had promised His servant, Abraham.

However, it is what Jacob said when he *"woke up from his sleep"* that immediately caught my attention. When he woke up he said, *"God is in this place and I did not know it!"* We will examine this powerful statement, but before we do, let us take an inventory of what was in the "place" where he slept.

- ❖ God Most High was in this sacred place.

- ❖ A great company of holy angels was stationed at this sacred place. The fact that the angels were ascending and descending on the ladder implies that the angels were already stationed at this place before he arrived.

- ❖ The Covenant of Abraham was very much alive and active in this place.

- ❖ The Glory of God was in this place.

But when Jacob awoke from his slumber, he was stunned by what he had discovered. He declares in utter awe and disbelief, "God is in this place and I did not know it!" Jacob's expression sadly describes the spiritual condition of much of the Church today. *The glory and reality of the living God is all around us but we lack the "consciousness" needed to relate and respond to His glory.* So we grapple in darkness and shoot at the wind with meaningless religious rituals that are designed to make us look spiritual, while God longs for us to experience His true glory. -Like Jacob of old, many believers are busy scheming to get ahead in their prophetic destiny using the arm of the flesh. But God desires to show us everything that He has already made available to us in His Kingdom if we can only relate to Him in "consciousness." Jacob's life changed dramatically when his spirit came into "consciousness" concerning the reality and glory of the living God. *Jacob started to draw on the deposit of God's Glory that was in this sacred place immediately after he became aware that he was surrounded by Glory.* Many members of the Body of Christ are not making withdrawals on their heavenly bank accounts, because they lack "consciousness" concerning the reality of the living God.

When we examine the sum total of everything that we have discussed in this chapter, it is easy to see why demonic powers love to strip people in the world as well as born-again believers of the mantle of biblical "consciousness." *Consciousness is at the heart of a dynamic spiritual life.* No one can have an accurate and robust spiritual walk with God if they lack the consciousness to relate to the glory and reality of the living God. *Consciousness separates facts from fiction, lies from truth and supernatural wisdom from mere human reasoning.* Many demonically engineered movies created by Hollywood movie producers with a godless agenda, are designed to strip moviegoers of consciousness, by making the abnormal acceptable, and casting a disapproving shadow over God sanctioned morality. It is my prayer that as you read this book, you will strengthen your resolve not to lose the *"War on Consciousness"* in your life to the demonic powers.

LIFE APPLICATION SECTION

MEMORY VERSE

Behold, I am with you and will keep you wherever you go, and will bring you back to this land; for I will not leave you until I have done what I have spoken to you." [16] *Then Jacob awoke from his sleep and said, "Surely the Lord is in this place, and I did not know it"*

(Genesis 28:15-16, NKJV).

1. What is the War on Consciousness?

2. How can Consciousness help you relate to the Glory and reality of the Living God?

Chapter Two

DEFINING CONSCIOUSNESS

Jesus said, "At my Father's direction I have done many good works. For which one are you going to stone me?" 33They replied, "We're stoning you not for any good work, but for blasphemy! You, a mere man, claim to be God." 34Jesus replied, "It is written in your own Scriptures that God said to certain leaders of the people, 'I say, you are gods!'35And you know that the Scriptures cannot be altered. So if those people who received God's message were called 'gods,' 36why do you call it blasphemy when I say, 'I am the Son of God'? After all, the Father set me apart and sent me into the world

(John 10:32-36).

The above passage of Scripture clearly demonstrates the tragedy of the lack of biblical consciousness. *Yeshua's audacious claim that He was the Son of God almost got Him stoned to death.* To avoid being stoned unnecessarily Yeshua defended Himself by referring to an Old Testament passage of Scripture from the book of Psalms. He told religious zealots who were plotting His murder to consider the fact that King David told the children of Israel of his era that they were gods - children of the Most High! Jesus proceeded to rebuke them by saying, *"If David could call the people who received God's message "gods" why would they be upset with his claims of divine Sonship?"* Put into another context, Yeshua was letting them know that their problem had nothing to do with His claims of divine Sonship. Their real problem was their lack of "consciousness." Stripped of "consciousness" by the demonic powers, they had forgotten that they had a God-given claim on divine sonship. We will now examine the passage from the Psalms that the Lord Jesus Christ referenced here.

God standeth in the congregation of the mighty; he judgeth among the gods.... ⁵They know not, neither will they understand; they walk on in darkness: all the foundations of the earth are out of course. ⁶I have said, Ye are gods; and all of you are children of the most High. ⁷But ye shall die like men, and fall like one of the princes

(Psalms 82:1,5-7, KJV).

King David, the beloved poet, psalmist, prophet and king of Israel, is given a startling prophetic vision. In this prophetic vision, God is standing in the midst of the congregation of the mighty ones. What is of note here is that the "mighty ones" being referenced here are the children of God. It is sad to see just how many children of God suffer from a shattered self-esteem. Through constant assault against their soul, the demonic powers have stripped them of consciousness concerning who they are in Christ. For the most part, they wallow in an unending cycle of self-pity. They daydream throughout the day wishing they were someone else. What a travesty!

YOU ARE GODS

King David's prophetic vision does not end in just declaring that we (the children of God) are the mighty ones, but it's what he says next that leaves most religious people tongue-tied. He declares that God's children (those who believe in God and His Christ) are gods! *How many religious Christians and Messianic Jews can handle this description of their proper estate in Christ Jesus?* You would be crucified in most Christian circles if you said, "I am a god." This is because the minds of so many people of faith have been brainwashed to believe that the term "gods" refers exclusively to the fallen demonic powers. *But this is a half-truth because the term "gods" in its original context is a reference to the children of the Most High God.* Greek and Roman mythology is filled with the worship of demons that the Greeks and Romans called "gods." Movies featuring demon gods that were worshipped in ancient Greece and Rome, such as "Zeus" have only served to promote the notion that the "gods" are the fallen demonic entities instead of the children of the Most High God. It is clear that only a person who is operating on a higher level of "consciousness" can acknowledge that they are "gods" (Children of the Most High) without feeling as if they are competing with God for deity. *God is in a class all by Himself and He is never threatened by the exaltation of His manifest sons into their proper estate. The deep cry for the manifestation of the sons of God that God has built into all of creation is further proof that God is not intimidated by the entrance of the New Creation into its god-like estate (see Romans 8:19-22).*

I am not suggesting that you go about telling anyone you meet that you are a "god." Even though you are truly a "god" in Christ Jesus! *I am merely using this powerful biblical expression to showcase just how much the Body of Christ has been stripped of consciousness concerning who they are in Christ in God!* The writer of the Psalms goes through a serious laundry list of social ills that plague the planet when the Children of the Most High God forget who they are. The psalmist lists the following ills that take place when children of God are stripped of consciousness concerning who "they are" in the *"ultimate reality and being" that we call God!*

❖ We will fail to give justice to the afflicted and oppressed.

❖ We will walk in darkness (Satan's domain) through the ignorance that is in our mind concerning our rightful inheritance in Christ.

❖ The spiritual, moral, financial and judicial foundations of the earth are forced out of guilt.

❖ The Children of the Most High God, though they are highly exalted in God's eyes, will live and die as mere men. Stripped of consciousness, the Children of the Most High God live out the rest of their life here on earth struggling with the mundane, instead of walking in the supernatural power of God!

DEFINING CONSCIOUSNESS

We will now begin to define biblical consciousness, so that you can wrap your mind around it. It is difficult to defend and protect what you cannot easily define.

1. *Consciousness is the tangible embodiment of a revelation that a person has come to believe and trust so completely that acting in accordance to that revelation is first nature to the said person.*

We will now examine this aspect of "Consciousness" that relates to "revelation" in order to give you a deeper understanding of our first definition of "Consciousness."

We proclaim to you the one who existed from the beginning, whom we have heard and seen. We saw him with our own eyes and touched him with our own hands. He is the Word of life. ²This one who is life itself was revealed to us, and we have seen him. And now we testify and proclaim to you that he is the one who is eternal life. He was with the Father, and then he was revealed to us. ³We proclaim to you what we ourselves have actually seen and heard so that you may have fellowship with us. And our fellowship is with the Father and with his Son, Jesus Christ. ⁴We are writing these things so that you may fully share our joy

(1 John 1:1-4).

In the above passage, John the beloved addresses the question of "consciousness" that wraps itself around a person's spirit and soul as an abiding unshakeable revelation. John lists the following reasons that transformed the knowledge of "Christ Jesus" as the "Word of life" into an unshakeable state of consciousness that radically transformed his life.

- We have seen and heard!

- We have seen "Him" with our naked eyes!

- We have touched "Him" with our bare hands!

- We have experienced "Him" as the Word of life!

- We have experienced "Him" as eternal life!

- We have experienced "Him" as the Joy of the Lord!

- What we have experienced and received from "Him" is so "real to us" we feel compelled to "share or proclaim it" to you!

What John the beloved apostle is declaring in the above passage of Scripture is that Christ Jesus, as the "One" all creation revolves around, was no longer just a powerful revelation in his life, but a very compelling, controlling, overwhelming experience of "consciousness." When any Kingdom citizen reaches this point of conviction concerning any revelation from Scripture, acting in accordance to that revelation becomes "first nature to them." At this point, that particular revelation turns into "consciousness." *A lot of biblical truths that many members of the Body of Christ purport to believe are never fully processed into the very fabric of their being until the truths become consciousness.* As a result, many of the biblical truths to which many in Christendom aspire, never become "first nature" in their lives. This explains why many people of faith fall into a place of compromise when confronted by circumstances that are contrary to the revelation they purport to believe. I know this is the case, because when many followers of Christ are placed in a "compelling setting" of compromise, they normally tilt towards compromising the truth they have championed publicly!

This also explains why Peter began to sink after walking on water for a while. When the disciples saw Jesus walking on the water, their initial (first nature) response was to proclaim, "It is a ghost!" Yeshua's disciples' initial reaction proves, that even though they were living with Him daily, their "first nature" consciousness was a "demonically engineered consciousness." *They believed that it was more probable for a ghost (a demonic entity) to walk on water instead of an angel of God.* But when they realized it was Jesus, Peter was the first to recover from the shock. He asked the Lord to prove His divinity by bidding him to walk on water.

Yeshua met Peter's challenge head on and bid him come. Peter stepped out of the boat and began to walk on water to the utter amazement of the other disciples. Unfortunately, the experience, though exhilarating, did not last long. Even though the experience of walking on water was a fresh, exciting revelation to Peter, it had not yet become consciousness. Consequently, as soon as the enemy began to sow seeds of doubt in his head about the validity of his new experience, Peter began to entertain second thoughts. The thoughts may have come like this: *"I am an ordinary* man. *What am I doing walking on water on the high seas! This is crazy. It may be okay for Yeshua but I am just an ordinary Jewish fisherman. What if the Word Yeshua gave me stops working and I drown? What is going to happen to my family then?"* Suddenly he began to sink and Yeshua reached out to save him but rebuked him sternly. Yeshua said, *"Why did you doubt me?"* Unfortunately, Peter's experience is not an isolated incident. Jesus is constantly asking the same question to many of His followers, "Why did you doubt me?" To my shame, He has asked me this same question over the years.

But why do many followers of Christ doubt Him when they are sick? Why do they doubt Him when they are faced with a pressing financial need? Before the Lord gave me the revelation on "Consciousness", I attributed this anomaly to mere human fragility. This was before I understood the vast difference between "revelation" and "consciousness." *Revelation is the unveiling of a new biblical truth through the power of the Holy Spirit. On the other hand, "Consciousness" is total immersion in the revelation that acting in accordance to that revelation becomes first nature to the person who believes in the revelation.* This is why I am now revisiting precious revelations given to me by the Holy Spirit from God's Word that I have never processed until they became "Consciousness." Walking on water was a powerful revelation for Peter, but walking on water was an overwhelming experience of consciousness for Yeshua! There is a vast difference between the two positions!

> *So they called the apostles back in and commanded them never again to speak or teach in the name of Jesus.* [19]*But Peter and John replied, "Do you think God wants us to obey you rather than him?* [20]*We cannot stop telling about everything we have seen and heard"*

(Acts 4:18-20).

Praise God! The above passage of Scripture demonstrates that Peter did eventually move on from revelation to consciousness! When the Sanhedrin council arrested Peter and John for preaching in the name of Yeshua, they were told to stop preaching in His name if they wished to live in peace. Faced with an imminent threat of physical harm, they had good reason for compromising. Fortunately, preaching Christ and Him crucified had grown from mere revelation to an overpowering feeling of consciousness. They could not act contrary to what they believed about the Messiah even if it meant losing their lives. Now, this is the vast difference between "consciousness and revelation!"

2. *Consciousness is the realization of the glory of God and the reality of the living God.*

We will now examine the aspect of "consciousness" that relates to the "glory and reality of the living of God" to give you a deeper understanding of our second definition of "consciousness."

About eight days later Jesus took Peter, John, and James up on a mountain to pray. 29And as he was praying, the appearance of his face was transformed, and his clothes became dazzling white. 30Suddenly, two men, Moses and Elijah, appeared and began talking with Jesus. 31They were glorious to see. And they were speaking about his exodus from this world, which was about to be fulfilled in Jerusalem

(Luke 9:28-31).

Perhaps there is no consciousness more important in the daily lives of God's people like the realization of the glory of God and the reality of the living God. Glory is the prevailing atmosphere of heaven. What makes heaven, heaven is that it is saturated with both the glory of God and the reality of the living God. Unfortunately, in most churches that have embraced the user-friendly gospel, live man-made entertainment has replaced the glory of the living God. This would explain why most congregants who attend these churches rarely have a working knowledge of the reality of the living God.

Knowing the importance of the glory of God and the reality of the living God in the propagation of the Gospel of the Kingdom, the Lord Jesus Christ took three of His prized disciples to the mountain of transfiguration. At the mountaintop, something supernatural and life changing transpired. The Bible tells us that while the Lord Jesus Christ was praying He was suddenly transfigured into the brightness of the glory of God. What is of note here is that the Transfiguration of the Lord Jesus Christ happened while He was praying fervently before God. The implied truth we can gather from this is that prayer is an important factor in the realization of the glory and the reality of the living God. This would explain why many prayer-less believers very seldom encounter the glory of God in their lives. The only winner in this scenario is the devil, who is terrified of a child of God sustaining a glory-consciousness.

As the glory of God engulfed the Lord Jesus Christ on the mountaintop, two very powerful Old Testament saints in the form of Moses and Elijah appeared in the glory and began to minister to Jesus. The Transfiguration of the Lord Jesus Christ on the mountaintop proved beyond any shadow of doubt that there is no distance or physical limitations in the glory. In the glory, there is no distance between heaven and earth. In the glory, the reality of the living God is an immutable fact. It is impossible to separate the glory of God from the reality of the living God.

Peter and the others had fallen asleep. When they woke up, they saw Jesus' glory and the two men standing with him. 33As Moses and Elijah were starting to leave, Peter, not even knowing what he was saying, blurted out, "Master, it's wonderful for us to be here! Let's make three shelters as memorials—one for you, one for Moses, and one for Elijah"

(Luke 9:32-33).

What is very interesting in the above passage of Scripture is that while the Lord Jesus Christ was having a supernatural encounter with the glory of God, His disciples were sound asleep. Unfortunately, the above scenario has repeated itself over the pages of church history; a church asleep in the midst of the glory of the living God. For the most part this sad state of affairs is quite common in the global Body of Christ. But, thank God, that Peter, James and John did not remain asleep for too long. The thunderous power of the glory of God awakened them into an adventure with Divinity that they would never forget for the rest of their lives. I truly believe that there is a spiritual awakening led by the Holy Spirit that is sweeping the Body of Christ worldwide. The Holy Spirit is about to birth a new consciousness in the global Body of Christ pertaining to the glory and reality of the living God. We are about to see the greatest demonstration of the Spirit and of power in the Body of Christ since the days of the apostles.

But even as he was saying this, a cloud overshadowed them, and terror gripped them as the cloud covered them. [35] *Then a voice from the cloud said, "This is my Son, my Chosen One. Listen to him"*

(Luke 9:34-35).

While the three disciples where captivated by the glory of God that was emanating from the Lord Jesus Christ, Moses and Elijah, another spectacular thing happened. The mesmerized disciples where suddenly introduced to the reality of the living God. An authoritative and majestic voice came tumbling out of the glory cloud. It was the voice of the Heavenly Father, validating His only begotten Son! There was no doubt that the heavenly Father loved the Son and was pleased with Him. This majestic voice from the cloud of glory forever changed the consciousness of the Apostle Peter to such an extent he never doubted the reality of the living God. Peter would later use this experience to validate both the gospel of Jesus Christ and his own apostleship. The Body of Christ desperately needs to understand the transforming power of consciousness that is rooted in the glory and reality of the Living God! This kind of consciousness will cause many members of the Body of Christ to live in the Glory Zone.

3. ***Consciousness is the awareness of the daily experience and interaction of your spirit and soul with the Holy Spirit.***

We will now examine the aspect of "Consciousness" that relates to the "awareness of the presence of the Holy Spirit" to give you a deeper understanding of our third definition of "Consciousness."

> *Next Paul and Silas traveled through the area of Phrygia and Galatia, because the Holy Spirit had prevented them from preaching the word in the province of Asia at that time. ⁷Then coming to the borders of Mysia, they headed north for the province of Bithynia, but again the Spirit of Jesus did not allow them to go there. ⁸So instead, they went on through Mysia to the seaport of Troas. ⁹That night Paul had a vision: A man from Macedonia in northern Greece was standing there, pleading with him, "Come over to Macedonia and help us!" ¹⁰So we decided to leave for Macedonia at once, having concluded that God was calling us to preach the Good News there*

(Acts 16:6-10).

When the Lord Jesus Christ announced His return to heaven, His announcement was received with mixed feelings by His band of disciples. Yeshua, sensing the somberness His announcement had created in the spirits of His disciples, made another equally powerful statement. He told His disciples that if He did not leave, the Comforter, the Holy Spirit, would not come. The ascension of the Lord Jesus Christ to the right hand of God would trigger the release of the ministry of the Holy Spirit to our ransomed planet until the consummation of the ages in Christ Jesus. True to His word, the Lord Jesus Christ baptized His band of disciples with the Holy Spirit and fire on the day of Pentecost.

Since the advent of the Holy Spirit on the day of Pentecost, the most important consciousness for living a truly successful life in the Kingdom of God is the daily interaction with the Holy Spirit. In the above passage of Scripture, the Bible tells us that Paul and Silas were forbidden by the Holy Spirit to preach the word of God in the province of Asia at that particular time. This is a very interesting statement to me because I was raised in a church culture where we were taught that it is okay to preach the word of God anywhere at any time. But the above passage of Scripture from the book of Acts flies against this conventional wisdom. It is clear from this passage that there are times when preaching the word of God to certain individuals and regions, without the leading of the Holy Spirit, can actually stifle the spiritual breakthrough of those regions or individuals. Approaching them before the soil of their hearts is ready to receive the gospel of Jesus Christ makes them more resistant to the gospel. This is why we need to develop the kind of consciousness that allows us to be both aware of the presence of the Holy Spirit and His daily interaction with our regenerated spirit. Without this daily awareness of the presence and person of the Holy Spirit, we will fall prey to the ploys of our carnal minds and end up becoming victims of the enemy. Perhaps this is the reason why the Bible declares in the book of Romans that as many as are led by the Spirit of God they are the sons of God.

Even though the Holy Spirit forbade Paul and Silas from speaking to the people of Asia about the gospel of the Kingdom, the Spirit visited Paul in a dream to give him his next assignment. In Paul's prophetic dream, he saw a man from Macedonia beseeching him for help. When he was wide-awake, Paul shared the prophetic dream with Silas and they both concluded that God was sending them to Macedonia to preach the gospel. This decision to preach in Macedonia instead of Asia proved to be a history changing strategic decision. Paul and Silas proceeded to preach in Macedonia where they were beaten and then sent to prison for preaching the gospel. At about midnight while they were in prison, Paul and Silas began to praise God, and the Bible says that the foundations of the prison were shaken by the power of God. The power of God shook the prison to such an extent that all the prison doors were opened and the chains of all the prisoners fell off. The Philippian jailer tried to kill himself before the Apostle Paul stopped him. The jailer gave his life to the Lord and became the pastor of the Macedonian church. By being aware of the presence and daily interaction with the Holy Spirit, the apostle Paul was able to follow the leading of the Holy Spirit all the way to a prison cell.

What is of note here is that Paul the apostle, was actually a Roman citizen. According to their law, no Roman citizen was ever to be subjected to punishment without trial or due process. While Paul and Silas were being beaten by the Macedonians for preaching the gospel, the apostle Paul deliberately hid the fact that he was a Roman citizen. Why would he do that? I believe it's because he knew from the prophetic dream that the Holy Spirit gave him that the man in his dream was the Macedonian jailer. The apostle and his companion were willing to accept temporary imprisonment in order to reach this strategic man for the gospel. Paul could have simply revealed his Roman citizenship while being beaten, and he would have been a free man. But the Apostle Paul was in such a place of consciousness, that he was aware of the presence of the Holy Spirit in his imprisonment. I believe that this type of consciousness of the daily awareness of the presence of the Holy Spirit and His interaction with our regenerated spirit will become an important spiritual technology in the end-time army of the Lord.

He remained there blind for three days and did not eat or drink. ¹⁰*Now there was a believer in Damascus named Ananias. The Lord spoke to him in a vision, calling, "Ananias!" "Yes, Lord!" he replied.* ¹¹*The Lord* said, "Go over to Straight Street, to the house of Judas. When you get there, ask for a man from Tarsus named Saul. He is praying to me right now. ¹²I have shown him a vision of a man named Ananias coming in and laying hands on him so he can see again." ¹³"But Lord," exclaimed Ananias, "I've heard many people talk about the terrible things this man has done to the believers in Jerusalem! ¹⁴And he is authorized by the leading priests to arrest everyone who calls upon your name." ¹⁵But the Lord said, "Go, for Saul is my chosen instrument to take my message to the Gentiles and to kings, as well as to the people of Israel. ¹⁶And I will show him how much he must suffer for my name's sake." ¹⁷So Ananias went and found Saul. He laid his hands on him and said, "Brother Saul, the Lord Jesus, who appeared to you on the road, has sent me so that you might regain your sight and be filled with the Holy Spirit." ¹⁸Instantly something like scales fell from Saul's eyes, and he regained his sight. Then he got up and was baptized

(Acts 9:9-18).

In the above passage of Scripture we will go deeper into examining the aspect of "consciousness" that relates to the *"daily awareness of the presence of the Holy Spirit and His interaction with our regenerated spirit."* Paul's dramatic encounter with the Lord Jesus Christ is duly noted in Scripture and in the annals of church history. Paul was on his way to Damascus with a decree from the high priest to either kill or imprison the people of the way. Paul was convinced that these born-again believers who were following Yeshua were a plague on Judaism. He considered it his personal mission to stop the spread of this plague in Israel. But on his way to Damascus, a blinding light struck him off his horse. While he was on the ground, the voice of the Lord Jesus Christ asked him why he was persecuting Him. From that moment, the apostle Paul was a changed man, but the Lord placed a temporary blindness over his eyes. His petrified companions dragged him into Damascus and left him in the house of a man called Judas. Once he was settled in Damascus, Paul began to fast and pray for three days. While he was fasting, the Lord showed him in a vision that He was going to send him another believer by the name of Ananias who was going to open his blind eyes.

Meanwhile, on the other side of this amazing story, the Lord was speaking to a disciple by the name of Ananias. The Lord told Ananias to go to Straight Street to the house of Judas where he would find a blind man by the name of Saul of Tarsus. In great trepidation, Ananias asked the Holy Spirit whether this Saul of Tarsus was the same as the Saul of Tarsus notorious for killing believers in Yeshua. The Lord quickly confirmed Ananias' great fear that it was the same Saul of Tarsus that God was sending them to. When Ananias tried to reason with the

Lord, the Lord explained to him further that Saul of Tarsus was now a changed man. God told Ananias that He was going to use Paul to bring the gospel to kings of nations. Ananias faithfully obeyed the voice of the Lord and went to Straight Street to Judas' house; and, sure enough, he found Paul grappling with blindness and he prophesied over him. The Lord supernaturally restored Paul's eyesight. The point I want to drive home by using this story is how it reveals the high level of consciousness that Ananias as a believer was operating under. Even though he was personally petrified of confronting such an infamous killer of believers, he went and did as the Lord instructed. Who does such a thing, unless they are definitely aware of the daily interactions of the Holy Spirit with their spirit? But unfortunately, this razor-sharp daily awareness of the presence of the Holy Spirit and His interaction with our spirit is sadly lacking in the lives of multiplied thousands of God's people.

4. ***Consciousness is the realization of the original you in Christ in God before all the man-made and demonically engineered programming was superimposed on your person.*** (See Colossians 3:1-4; Jeremiah 1:1-5.)

We will now examine the aspect of "consciousness" that relates to the "realization of the original YOU" to give you a deeper understanding of our fourth definition of "consciousness."

Since you have been raised to new life with Christ, set your sights on the realities of heaven, where Christ sits in the place of honor at God's right hand. ²Think about the things of heaven, not the things of earth. ³For you died to this life, and your real life is hidden with Christ in God (Colossians 3:1-4).

The legendary Christian author, C.S. Lewis, said that the greatest gift God ever gave to mankind is the gift to be ourselves. Unfortunately, we live in a world where corporations and politicians are trying aggressively to reprogram us to suit their own ends. All you have to do is switch on television and you will be ambushed by thousands of advertisements, each fighting for position in our consciousness so that we can march to the drumbeat of people sending the programming signals. This is why the subject of consciousness is so important: it is the well being of the spiritual life of a child of God.

One key aspect of consciousness is the realization of the original "YOU" in Christ in God before all the man-made and demonically engineered programming was superimposed on your person. God creates every human being with a specific purpose. Consequently, when a person is born they are not a mistake because God has ordained them for a purpose that they are to fulfill here on earth. Unfortunately, many of us are raised in homes where the majority of our parents have no understanding of divine destiny. Most of our parents do not understand the purpose of God for their own life, let alone ours. Consequently, they fashion and program their children to conform to their environment instead of who they are in Christ in God. The above passage tells us that all born-again believers have died to their old life. This is why I believe that the primary work of the Holy Spirit is to show us who we once were in Christ in God before we arrived on this planet. When we come into this type of consciousness, it is impossible not to live a purpose-driven life. For instance, Jacob was actually Israel, a prince, who had power with both God and man and yet he lived the first part of his life as a supplanter, because this was the meaning of the name Jacob. But at the river Jabok (Genesis 32), God changed his name from Jacob to Israel. Israel, and not Jacob, is who he was in Christ in God before he came into this world. As soon as God returned him to his original estate, he quickly flourished into Israel the beloved nation of God. The name Israel bestowed upon him a new consciousness that ignited his true self.

> *"I knew you before I formed you in your mother's womb. Before you were born I set you apart and appointed you as my prophet to the nations."* *⁶"O Sovereign Lord," I said, "I can't speak for you! I'm too young!" ⁷The Lord replied, "Don't say, 'I'm too young,' for you must go wherever I send you and say whatever I tell you"*

(Jeremiah 1:5-7).

The above passage of Scripture from the book of Jeremiah is probably one of the most powerful Old Testament passages on the issue of consciousness as it relates to our ability to relate to who we once were in Christ in God before we came into this world. The Lord approaches young Jeremiah and tells him "before I formed you in your mother's womb I knew you." In other words, God in His foreknowledge had an intimate knowledge of who young Jeremiah was created to be even before his parents conceived him. The Lord tells young Jeremiah that even before he was born the Lord had already set him apart and appointed him as a prophet to the nations. Unfortunately, young Jeremiah did not see such potential in himself. He had become reprogrammed by his environment and by the demonic powers. He began to tell the Lord that he couldn't speak and that he was too young to be a prophet to the nations. But the Lord rebuked him for saying such a thing. He told him that age could not define who he was in Christ in God before he came to this planet. But it is clear from Jeremiah's response that he was suffering from a different type of programming than the one the Lord had bestowed upon him before he came to this planet. For all practical purposes, the spirit of young Jeremiah had forgotten who he once was in Christ in God.

The first chapter of the book of Jeremiah truly fascinates me, because it clearly demonstrates that in each person (saved or unsaved) there is a "YOU" that God formed and fashioned before we came to this planet. I call this aspect of mankind, the original "YOU" in Christ in God from before the foundation of the world. But this original "YOU" has a formidable challenger: the demonic, fallen program or self, known as "I." Several times in the above passage, Jeremiah challenged the eternal wisdom of God by referring to himself as "I." This was the same type of expression that destroyed the devil and caused one third of the holy angels to fall with him. It is clear that the devil's favorite talk is "me, myself and I." True consciousness is our only hope against such a malicious demonic program. This is the aspect of consciousness that I am praying the Lord would give to you as you read this book. The consciousness which is a result of our realization of our original "self" in Christ in God is the only one that can set us free from our man made identity and self-worth.

DEACTIVATING THE I-PROGRAM

"I knew you before I formed you in your mother's womb. Before you were born I set you apart and appointed you as my prophet to the nations." ⁶*"O Sovereign Lord," I said, "I can't speak for you! I'm too young!"* ⁷*The Lord replied, "Don't say, 'I'm too young,' for you must go wherever I send you and say whatever I tell you.* ⁸*And don't be afraid of the people, for I will be with you and will protect you. I, the Lord, have spoken!"* ⁹*Then the Lord reached out and touched my mouth and said, "Look, I have put my words in your mouth!* ¹⁰*Today I appoint you to stand up against nations and kingdoms. Some you must uproot and tear down, destroy and overthrow. Others you must build up and plant"*

(Jeremiah 1:4-10).

The above passage from the book of Jeremiah is one of the most classic examples of the greatest hindrance to a complete return to consciousness. We will address this number one hindrance to consciousness in this section of the book. In the famed movie, *The Matrix* Morpheus the prophet from the City of Zion confronts young Neal with a staggering choice. He shows him a red and blue pill. He told him that he could only have one of the pills, so he had to choose wisely. Young Neal asks Morpheus what the two pills represent and Morpheus' answer is very applicable to our discussion on consciousness. Morpheus tells Neal that if he chose the blue pill he would return to the life he was familiar with. A seemingly safe and predictable life trapped in a false reality called the "Matrix." A malicious program called "the agents" controlled the people who lived in the matrix. On the other hand, if he chose the "red pill" he would come into a "new and higher level of consciousness" that would deliver him from that false reality called the "matrix" and allow him to discover his true "self."

In the movie, Neal made what proved, in the end, to be the right choice. *He chose the red pill. He immediately became "unplugged" from the false reality of the matrix to eventually become the savior of Zion. In his new state of consciousness, Neal realized that the life he had known in the matrix was not as "safe" as he had supposed.* To the contrary, it was the most dangerous life a human being could ever live. This is because the people who lived in the "false reality" called the matrix, were actually pawns of a malicious program called "the agents" (demons). These people were not as free and safe as they thought they were. They were actually asleep to their true purpose and potential. Even though *The Matrix* is a fictional movie made by Hollywood, the Lord spoke to me through it. He said to me, "the blue pill" represents sin, which binds the people of our planet to a false sense of reality. These people who are sedated on the blue pill are being remotely controlled by demonic entities (Satan's agents). On the other hand, the "red pill" represents the precious blood of Jesus. The blood of Jesus is the only agent in the universe that can unplug lost souls from the false reality of the matrix. Applying the blood of Christ over our heart and mind is the beginning of a new and higher state of consciousness.

In the above passage from the book of Jeremiah, an interesting conversation between God and young Jeremiah ensues. What comes out of this conversation underscores the greatest hindrance to coming into a heightened state of consciousness. God tells Jeremiah, "Before I formed "YOU" in your mother's womb I knew "YOU" and ordained "YOU" as a prophet to the nations!" [Emphasis added] *You would think that Jeremiah would have started shouting in celebration but instead he recoiled in fear.* Instead, he tells God, *"I am a child. Behold I cannot speak."* What we quickly observe from the divine conversation between God and Jeremiah is the clear drawing of the battle lines. *The battle lines are drawn around two very competing programs, one divine and the other demonic.* The divine program was a "YOU" program and the demonic program was an "I" program.

THE I-PROGRAM VERSUS THE ORIGINAL YOU

God, who cannot lie and knows all things, declares to Jeremiah that before *"I formed "YOU" in your mother's womb, I knew "YOU."* So we see that there was a "YOU" in young Jeremiah that God formed and foreknew in His foreknowledge. *This "YOU" that was trapped in Jeremiah represented "his true self," without the influence of demonically engineered programing.* God went further and informed Jeremiah that this "YOU" in him was the "YOU" that had the potential to become a prophet of God to the nations. This "YOU" *was not restricted in consciousness by age, space or time.* Unleashing this "YOU" that was trapped in Jeremiah would set him free from living inside the false reality of the matrix. *Unfortunately, another very malicious, demonically engineered program was also operating in young Jeremiah.* It was the "I" program. This demonic program places "self" (I) in the place where God is supposed to be. This demonic program says, *"I can`t," where God says, "I can!"* This demonic program first appeared in Lucifer and transformed him into Satan (see Isaiah 14:12-15). This "I" program is a slave of the law of sin and death. Failure to break free of this demonically engineered program will doom us to a life of sin and death. *This program is single handedly the greatest hindrance to living in a higher level of consciousness!* It is my prayer that God will deliver you from this demonic program as you are reading this book.

THE QUESTION OF IDENTITY THEFT

When the Holy Spirit revealed to me the stark difference between the "YOU" and "I" programs, it suddenly dawned on me why many followers of Christ are wrestling with the frustration that comes from having too many unfulfilled prophecies in their lives. I have come across many believers who have told me that they do not wish to listen to one more prophecy when their journal is full of prophecies they received from notable prophets that have not yet materialized. I understand their frustration and sympathize with them because I was also on a personal quest to discover the answer to the question of unfulfilled prophecy. But when the Lord showed me the difference between the "YOU" and "I" program, the answer to the mystery was suddenly revealed to me.

The Holy Spirit showed me that the answer to the dilemma of unfulfilled prophecy is rooted in dealing with a question of "Identity Theft." *The Lord told me that when the Holy Spirit releases a personal prophecy over any individual the prophecy is always directed towards the "original YOU" in Christ in God!* The prophetic Word is the property of your regenerated human spirit not the outward man that everybody sees. *If the truth were told, many Christians are not walking in their "true self" but in a self that for the most part has been programmed by culture, the environment and the invisible influence of the demonic powers.* Consequently, when many sincere followers of Christ receive a prophecy they immediately apply it to the "I" that they know themselves to be, when in actuality the prophecy was addressed to their inward man (spirit). Sadly, many Christians are so "soulish" their "spirit man" rarely comes out of the shell of their persona to do the work of God! Consequently, their "soulish persona" superimposes itself over prophetic words that the LORD meant to be assumed by the regenerated spirit. In the daily grind of life, this phenomenon is known as "identity theft."

I asked God to give me a clear biblical example of this phenomenon and He did. He took me to the book of Genesis. The Bible tells us that while Rebekah was pregnant she felt a tug of war in her womb. She inquired of the Lord why this was so. The Lord gave her a powerful prophecy of things to come. The Lord said...

> *Isaac pleaded with the Lord on behalf of his wife, because she was unable to have children. The Lord answered Isaac's prayer, and Rebekah became pregnant with twins. ²²But the two children struggled with each other in her womb. So she went to ask the Lord about it. "Why is this happening to me?" she asked. ²³And the Lord told her, "The sons in your womb will become two nations. From the very beginning, the two nations will be rivals. One nation will be stronger than the other; and your older son will serve your younger son." ²⁴ And when the time came to give birth, Rebekah discovered that she did indeed have twins! 25 The first one was very red at birth and covered with thick hair like a fur coat. So they named him Esau. ²⁶Then the other twin was born with his hand grasping Esau's heel. So they named him Jacob. Isaac was sixty years old when the twins were born*

(Genesis 25:21-26).

When the two children were born, Rebekah took notice of the child who came out last because of the prophecy that God gave her concerning the inherent destinies of her two sons. Isaac, who did not understand God's original intent for his younger son, gave him a name that was contrary to his inherent destiny. Isaac named his second son, "Jacob," which means "supplanter." But the child's "true self" in Christ in God answered to the name "Israel." *The prophecy that God had given to Rebekah over her younger son was never meant for "Jacob"; it was intended for "Israel."* "Jacob" was who he was naturally. But "Israel" was what he became when God restored his "consciousness" concerning his true self in Christ in God. The supernatural encounter he had with God at the Jabbok River challenged his perceived identity as "Jacob" and restored him to his true identity in God's Kingdom as "Israel." As "Jacob," he remained a supplanter, deceiver, hustler and God only knows what else. But as "Israel," he was a prince endued with the power to prevail with God and man.

During the night Jacob got up and took his two wives, his two servant wives, and his eleven sons and crossed the Jabbok River with them. [23] After taking them to the other side, he sent over all his possessions. [24] This left Jacob all alone in the camp, and a man came and wrestled with him until the dawn began to break. [25] When the man saw that he would not win the match, he touched Jacob's hip and wrenched it out of its socket. [26] Then the man said, "Let me go, for the dawn is breaking!" But Jacob said, "I will not let you go unless you bless me." [27] "What is your name?" the man asked. He replied, "Jacob." [28] "Your name will no longer be Jacob," the man told him. "From now on you will be called Israel because you have fought with God and with men and have won"

(Genesis 32:21-28).

In his fleshly and demonically engineered effort to fulfill the prophecy that God spoke over his life before he was born, Jacob supplanted his elder brother of his firstborn birthright. When Isaac told Esau to go into the wild to hunt for a wild animal so he could bless him, Jacob, in tandem with his mother, devised the most devious plan to steal the blessing from unsuspecting Esau. *The scheme they concocted was the most devious case of "Identity Theft" ever mentioned in Scripture.* I do not have the space to focus on the scheme they concocted, except to say it involved Jacob pretending to be Esau in front of his father who was blind for all practical purposes. When Esau discovered that his scheming brother had supplanted him, a spirit of murder came upon him. When Jacob saw that his life was in danger he fled into exile.

On his way to Syria to live with his uncle Laban, he slept at a place called Luz. While he was sleeping, he dreamed of a ladder that reached up to Heaven. He saw angels ascending and descending on this ladder. At the top of the ladder, he saw the Lord. God spoke to him. He told him that He would bless him and his descendants with the land he was sleeping on. When Jacob "woke up", he was deeply moved and made a very interesting statement.

Then Jacob awoke from his sleep and said, "Surely the Lord is in this place, and I wasn't even aware of it!"

(Genesis 28:16).

When Jacob woke-up he said, *"The Lord is in this place and 'I' did not know it!"* Jacob confessed that he couldn't really discern the Lord's presence when the "I" program was active in him. But why did the Lord wait until he was asleep before He appeared to him? The reason is staggeringly simple:

God uses dreams while people sleep to bypass the demonic programing that makes it difficult for most Christians to hear from God while they are awake. God uses dreams to speak to our "true self," because when many of us are awake, the demonic "I" program is very active. The Lord told me that at the City of Luz (later known as Bethel) God put Jacob to sleep so He could speak to "Israel" who was still trapped in Jacob! *The prophecies that Jacob thought were his actually belonged to "Israel."* The name "Jacob" represented the supplanting nature of the flesh, while the name "Israel" represented the life-giving divine nature of God! When he became Israel, he began to manifest the prophecy that God gave to his mother before he was born. He suddenly became greater in spiritual stature than his elder brother. While he remained "Jacob," Esau had the power to place him in exile but as soon as he became "Israel," Esau was placed in total subjection! *This is what coming into "consciousness" will do for millions of Christians around the world who have endured perennial defeat at the hands of the enemy!*

SUMMARY

Consciousness is the original you, the one without all the programming or thoughts that you have allowed to influence your life. This "YOU," was created with the sole purpose of living for God's pleasure and for seeking Him. This is the part of you that can have true communion with God. The other parts, thoughts, emotions can be manipulated and deceived. The real "YOU" only surfaces to seek God's face. You can choose to be locked away, hence enabling other aspects to rule "who" you really are. These other aspects can include institutions, other people, spirits and even demons.

Terms like universal consciousness and global consciousness relate to group or global connectedness and have nothing to do with the CONSCIOUSNESS that I am referring to here. Universal and global consciousness are simply higher forms of awareness, but in no way relate to consciousness. Consciousness is man's ability to realize who and what he is. Consciousness is the realization of a sinful nature; the "programmed supposed you" aspect and your continuous onslaught against it to be a spiritually-minded person. Consciousness goes hand in hand with awakening or rebirth of the real YOU, by the Holy Spirit. Consciousness is not, to be fleshly-minded, but rather refers to being a spiritually-minded person, as Paul references in the Bible. (Excerpt from www. stopfollowingman.org)

LIFE APPLICATION SECTION

MEMORY VERSE

Behold, I am with you and will keep you wherever you go, and will bring you back to this land; for I will not leave you until I have done what I have spoken to you." 16Then Jacob awoke from his sleep and said, "Surely the Lord is in this place, and I did not know it" (Genesis 28:15-16, NKJV).

1. What is the I-Program and how does it relate to the subject of Consciousness?

2. How does rediscovering the original "YOU" in Christ in God help you in the battle for Consciousness?

Chapter Three

STRESS AND MORE STRESS

Consider the ravens, for they neither sow nor reap, which have neither storehouse nor barn; and God feeds them. Of how much more value are you than the birds? *²⁵And which of you by worrying can add one cubit to his stature?* *²⁶If you then are not able to do the least, why are you anxious for the rest?*

(Luke 12:24-26, NKJV).

We live in a world that is driven by the engines of chaos and unrest. In this world of chaos and unrest, people are constantly bombarded by situations that demand they enter the domain of stress. According to the *American Medical Journal*, stress has now become the number one killer in the United States of America surpassing cancer. Even stress-induced violent crimes are on the rise all over the world. Thousands of marriages, even those in Christendom, have also fallen victim to the menacing power of stress. Dealing with stress has become a multibillion-dollar industry. Understanding this trend, many pharmaceutical companies are working tirelessly to mass-produce stress-inhibiting drugs that are sold at ridiculous prices to generate outrageous profits. Unfortunately, these drug-induced stress inhibitors also create their own umbrella of problems and side effects.

In 2009, the world was shocked to learn of the death of one of the most famous music icons in history, Michael Jackson. Before his untimely death, it was common knowledge that the famous music icon and king of pop was addicted to prescription drugs. Most of these drugs were stress inhibitors designed to put him to sleep. But one day, Michael Jackson took one pill too many and never woke up again. Millions around the world mourned the death of the iconic singer, while examining their own mortality.

In the above passage of Scripture, the Lord Jesus Christ confronts the problem of stress head-on. Yeshua deals with the stress problem without beating about the bush. In the above passage of Scripture, Jesus deals a deathblow to our stress-driven culture, where worrying about tomorrow is king. In dealing with the problem of stress, the Lord Jesus Christ gives us an interesting framework to work with.

WHEN BIRDS TEACH

Firstly, Yeshua admonishes us to consider the ravens, or the birds, of the air. The word "consider" literally means, to examine thoroughly. This word "consider" in the text denotes the act of researching, investigating and analyzing a subject with forensic aptitude in order to apply the results of such a thorough study to our daily lives.

Secondly, Yeshua informs us that these ravens, or birds, do not sow nor reap. This is a very interesting comment because it demonstrates the advantage mankind has over the animal kingdom. Mankind can by divine election participate in one of the most powerful laws for creating a future of increase, *"the law of sowing and reaping."* Even though the ravens do not participate in this powerful law of increase, Yeshua tells us that our heavenly Father feeds these birds continually and none of these birds are being treated for stress at any medical facility.

After establishing the fact that the birds of the air do not sow or reap, the Lord Jesus Christ moves on and makes another very compelling argument. *This argument is based upon man's divine ranking of importance as compared to the birds of the air.* In God's divine ranking of importance, no creature in creation is more valuable to Him than mankind. So the argument Yeshua is making is simply this, *"If our Heavenly Father who ranks us much higher than the birds of the air is dedicated to feeding the birds of the air, to what extent is He willing to go to sustain His most prized possession?"*

A QUESTION THAT DEMANDS AN ANSWER

Yeshua does the final blow to our worry and stress-driven culture by asking us a question that demands our honest response. He asks, *"Which of us can add one more day to our life by worrying incessantly?"* In other words, the Messiah is saying, "Since many of us are perennial 'worriers,' what return have we ever received on our investment of worrying constantly?" Since the answer is obviously, "Nothing!" it would seem that the way of wisdom is to stop worrying about tomorrow or what we are going to eat and begin to trust God instead. In His foreknowledge, God has already provided for all our needs according to His riches in glory in Christ Jesus.

One day my wife was driving on a very busy highway in New York when suddenly she heard a screeching sound as if she was dragging something. She pulled over and found out that her muffler was on the highway because the screws holding it in place fell off. Her sister's boyfriend, Nick, who was with her said they needed a bungee cord, similar to those used by bikers, to temporarily secure the muffler until they could get to the nearest car repair shop. She answered and said she didn't have a bungee cord, but they could walk half a mile to get help from a gas station they just passed. My wife's sister and her boyfriend began to walk towards the gas station. To my wife's surprise, she saw them returning before they even reached the station. When they came back, Nick was smiling and nodding his head. In his hand was a bungee cord, which they found on the side of thehighway! Nick tied the muffler with the bungee cord and they were able to get to their destination without any problem. This shows that God already knew that at that very moment, my wife would need some help with her car and allowed somebody to leave a bungee cord a few meters from where they stopped. So when it comes to the issue of providing for His prized possession, the Heavenly Father has no close match.

ALL THINGS HAVE BEEN DELIVERED TO ME

All things have been delivered to Me by My Father, and no one knows the Son except the Father. Nor does anyone know the Father except the Son, and the one to whom the Son wills to reveal Him. ²⁸*Come to Me, all you who labor and are heavy laden, and I will give you rest.* ²⁹*Take My yoke upon you and learn from Me, for I am gentle and lowly in heart, and you will find rest for your souls.* ³⁰*For My yoke is easy and My burden is light"* **(Matthew 11:27-30, NKJV).**

The Lord Jesus makes another gigantic statement that carries with it very deep spiritual implications. He declares that the Heavenly Father has delivered "all things" into His hands. The phrase "all things" encompasses everything that exists within the scope of creation. This means that there is nothing in creation, including the devil and his kingdom, which are not included in "all things" that have been delivered into His hands. This gigantic statement needs to be digested for all its worth by followers of Christ everywhere. Digesting and understanding the vast implications of this gigantic statement by the Lord Jesus Christ will produce great peace of mind in the believers so exercised. Such a believer will find that overcoming stress and its insidious side effects becomes that much easier.

The Lord Jesus Christ makes another equally important statement in which He declares that no man knows the Heavenly Father except the Son and the person to whom the Son reveals Him. This statement by the Lord Jesus Christ is not designed to sound elitist but a mere statement of fact. The statement implies that we are not to believe the traditions or the lies of our culture concerning the true nature of the Heavenly Father outside the revelation of Him delivered to us by His Son. This means that any image of the Heavenly Father that contradicts what the Lord Jesus Christ has told us about the Heavenly Father and His eternal benevolence must not be believed. Many people in our culture, and even some Christians, have an image of the Heavenly Father that is much like some of their earthly fathers who were reluctant providers or painfully stingy. Consequently, many of these people stress and worry easily about the lack of provision thereof because they are not convinced that God is determined to meet their every need. Knowing that there are many flawed concepts and distorted images of the Heavenly Father, the Lord Jesus makes it clear in the text that He is the only One who has exclusivity in the arena of establishing the true image of the Heavenly Father. Consequently, if the Lord Jesus tells us that the Heavenly Father is so benevolent, He even takes care of the birds of the air, we can rest assured that He has already met every aspect of our provision light years before we encounter them.

COME TO ME

Come to Me, all you who labor and are heavy laden, and I will give you rest. *²⁹Take My yoke upon you and learn from Me, for I am gentle and lowly in heart, and you will find rest for your souls. ³⁰For My yoke is easy and My burden is light"(Matthew 11:28-30, NKJV).*

The Lord Jesus Christ gives us one of the most life changing invitations that has ever taken place between God and man. This invitation is our way out of a life driven by the engines of chaos and stress. The invitation starts with the expression *"Come to Me."* These three words are probably some of the most powerful words that a person who is stressed over life events can ever receive. The expression *"Come to Me"* is very direct but also diagnostic. It is diagnostic in the sense that the expression unmasks the central problem of man. Since the fall of Adam and Eve in the Garden of Eden, when they walked away from the presence of God, mankind has since developed many devious ways of running from God. Running away from God is a misguided reaction that in itself sentences men to a life of stress and ultimately death. The quickest way for mankind to be delivered from the burden of worry and stress is to run to God. This is what Jesus meant when He said, *"Come to Me."* It is an invitation to bring ourselves, and all that ails us, to the *'One being'* who can fix it all. But man's loss of his original consciousness robs him of the drive to run to God. Consequently, man has become a master of his own destruction by running to things of lower ranking than God to get his needs met. Even in the Body of Christ, many people are stressed out because they are spending their energy on Christian counseling and psychiatry instead of running into God's presence.

The Lord Jesus in this glorious invitation informs us that all labor of the spirit, soul and body outside His calming presence will only impose upon us many burdens. This would explain why very successful and wealthy people on our planet commit suicide after struggling with a nagging emptiness of the soul regardless of their immense wealth. Henceforth, the Lord's invitation is also an invitation out of that type of work in creation that causes us to struggle for provision with the sweat of our brow.

THE POWER OF REST

The Lord's invitation becomes that much sweeter when He promises to give us rest from all our burdens when we come to Him. Rest is the greatest need of man's triune nature: spirit, soul and body. Spiritual exhaustion has led many to walk away from the faith or from the ministry. Emotional and mental exhaustion can be just as devastating. The prisons of America and the world are filled with men that made life-altering decisions in times of emotional exhaustion. Physical exhaustion is even more dangerous. This is because in our triune nature, the flesh is the weakest link. This is what Jesus meant when He said, "the spirit is willing but the flesh is weak." Only the divorce courts and the lingering emotional scars left on children of divorced parents can tell the damaging effects of physical exhaustion. Many marriages ended just because the partners involved were physically exhausted from continually trying to make their marriage work. They no longer had the energy to work at it. A dear man of God that I respect once told me that when exhaustion sets in, faith walks out. Knowing all of this, the Lord invites us graciously to come to Him so He can give us rest. Why the promise of rest? The Lord promises "rest," because "rest" by its very divine nature demands that we engage a higher level of consciousness. Stress on the other hand vibrates at a very low frequency because it is the fruit of a much-diminished sense of consciousness. Stress, like all things of a lower nature, vibrates at a very low frequency. It is so easy for a person under stress to contract any kind of disease, including cancer, because all diseases have a low frequency resonance. Demons also have a low frequency resonance because they are far removed from the glorious light of God that vibrates at a very high frequency.

MY YOKE IS EASY

In the glorious invitation of the Lord Jesus Christ to fallen humanity, He promises to exchange the yoke of oppression upon our lives for His righteous yoke. In ancient times, a yoke was a crooked stick that was placed around the neck of cattle in order to guide them as they plowed a field. The yoke of the Lord speaks of the guiding power of His Lordship. We were never created to lord it over others or ourselves. Such a life can only lead to misery, death and destruction. Whether men realize it or not, the restlessness in their souls can never be healed by things but by the yoke of His Lordship. Much of Christian experience proves this point very clearly. I have talked to both men and women who spoke to me teary-eyed and told me just how much peace came upon them when they gave their life to Christ. Many of them attest to how they almost destroyed themselves and their families when they were lords unto themselves. But it takes a higher level of consciousness to accept the Lord's Lordship, for the highest gift a man can give to God is the gift of himself. When we enter into a higher level of consciousness through the power of the Holy Spirit, we will discover that living under His Lordship is easy. It is truly life as God intended. God's Lordship over our spirit, soul and body is by far the most natural form of leadership that we can ever expose ourselves to. This is why the Apostle Paul declares in the book of Romans, *"For as many as are led by the Spirit, these are the sons of God"(8:14, NKJV)*.

In the Lord's glorious invitation, He further sweetens the deal by admonishing us to learn from Him. The phrase "learn of Me" is without doubt a very powerful pillar in the glorious invitation. The expression "learn of Me" has two very powerful implications. First, it implies that it is very possible for the followers of Christ to learn to walk in the Spirit in the exact same manner as Jesus did. This may be frightening to those with a religious mindset. But it is nevertheless the truth of the Scripture. If Jesus never believed that we could learn in the Spirit exactly as He did, making such an invitation would be most cruel. But such is not the case, because He became one of us in the incarnation so that we could be like Him in resurrection. This also means that we can learn to live in a heightened and unbroken level of consciousness that Jesus Christ exhibited while He was on earth.

LEARN OF ME

Secondly, the expression "learn of Me" also implies that we are forbidden to learn from any other whose foundation is not the Christ of God. This means that to live in the same heightened level of consciousness that Christ walked in, we cannot learn from Mohammed, Buddha or any other philosophers. This is what is so dangerous about the doctrine of universal reconciliation that states that God, as demonstrated in Christ, could be found in world religions that spit at the very mention of the Name of Jesus. Many Christians are living in an emotional wasteland because of trying to deal with the stress in their lives by learning from motivational gurus while neglecting the examples set in Christ. In learning from Him, we will discover how to stay at rest even in the midst of the storm. This is why Jesus slept peacefully in the midst of the worst storm they had ever gone through at sea, so that they could learn from Him.

GENTLE AND LOWLY IN HEART

In the glorious invitation to a life of peace and rest, the Lord makes the case for why we should learn from Him. It is because He is gentle and lowly in heart. This expression would seem to be out of place in a passage that promises us rest and a life free from stress. But the great King Solomon declares in the book of Proverbs that it is a soft answer that turns away wrath. It is my experience that when people are stressed out they tend to be verbally harsh. This is because when people are stressed out they usually are emotionally exhausted; so they run out of patience and, therefore, are "short at the mouth." But, unfortunately, harshness only begets more harshness, serving only to increase emotional stress as they fight with those close to them. Gentleness on the other hand serves great dividend and endears the emotional and spiritual support of those closest to them. Having the spiritual and emotional support of our peers goes a long way in eliminating stress. So far, we have only addressed the gentleness aspect of the expression we are studying; but what about Christ's claim of being lowly in heart? How does knowing this aid us in living a life of rest and void of stress? The expression "lowly in heart" speaks a deep abiding sense of humility that was in Christ Jesus. It is the testimony of Scripture that God resists the proud and gives grace to the humble. We cannot live a restful life void of stress when pride is our master. Pride opens the door for those insidious demonic technologies that cumulatively create pain and stress in our relationships. Humility on the other hand guarantees us a powerful standing before the presence of God.

MY BURDEN IS LIGHT

In closing, the Lord's glorious invitation ends with a very powerful summation as He declares, "My burden is light!" For a long time when I read this passage of Scripture, I immediately assumed that the burden that the Lord was referring to was measured in mass. So, in my mind, I had a picture of a man carrying a heavy load on his shoulder. And I saw the Lord come to him and take off the heavy load and replace it with a lighter load. But the Holy Spirit told me one day that this was not the case. Then I saw it.

The Lord Jesus Christ was not referring to a burden created by a weight with physical mass but to a very different type of burden. The burden in this instance that Christ places upon us is the burden of carrying "the light of revelation" in His Kingdom. It is the kind of burden of light that dispels the darkness so that we can see clearly. Imagine for a moment that you are sitting in a very dark room filled with all the resources that you need to dispel all your needs. While the darkness lingers you will stress heavily because the only knowledge you have at the time is the knowledge of your unmet needs. But let us imagine for a moment that a good Samaritan walks into the dark room and suddenly turns on the light. To your great dismay you discover that the room is filled with all the resources you have so desperately needed. In such a case, what do you think will happen to your stress? It will dissipate in seconds. It would be replaced by unspeakable joy and full of glory. In essence, when the Lord Jesus declares that His burden is light, He is actually inviting us in the same exact Sonship-consciousness that permeated every part of His being while He was on earth. For this same kind of Sonship-consciousness is truly the eternal destiny of the sons of God. The Apostle Paul entered this exact same level of consciousness in the latter part of his ministry on earth. This would explain why Paul did not stress or worry when a poisonous snake bit him, while he was on the Island of Miletus.. While the Islanders waited anxiously to see him dead, he went about his business as though nothing happened. The Islanders eventually concluded that he was a god when he cheated death. A revival of historic proportions took place thereafter.

LIFE APPLICATION SECTION

MEMORY VERSE

Consider the ravens, for they neither sow nor reap, which have neither storehouse nor barn; and God feeds them. Of how much more value are you than the birds? [25]*And which of you by worrying can add one cubit to his stature?* [26]*If you then are not able to do the least, why are you anxious for the rest?*

(Luke 12:24-26, NKJV).

1. What did Jesus mean when He said, "Come to Me"?

2. What is the burden of Light?

Chapter Four

THE POWER OF CONSCIOUSNESS

For all who are led by the Spirit of God are children of God. ¹⁵So you have not received a spirit that makes you fearful slaves. Instead, you received God's Spirit when he adopted you as his own children. Now we call him, "Abba, Father." ¹⁶For his Spirit joins with our spirit to affirm that we are God's children

(Romans 8:14-16).

Learning the art of unbroken communion with the precious Holy Spirit on a daily basis is undoubtedly the highest "consciousness." Without knowing the Holy Spirit, our journey into true consciousness will be derailed by the demonic powers that are desperate for men to attain consciousness without God.

CAN YOU HEAR THE HOLY SPIRIT?

Here is something to consider. Without being conscious or having consciousness, it is impossible to comprehend any of the more subtle levels of demonic influence operating in our world. Being stripped of consciousness would prevent you from being able to hear the Holy Spirit or feel His convictions. It would be like living a dream where the reality you perceive is in fact darkness, but it masquerades as light. Your malware or virus (that which has infected your conscious) is so deeply embedded that you no longer even have access to your consciousness. Someone else is operating your body but your loop, or the repetitive program placed in your mind assures you that you are fine; you are in control. Meanwhile, pride, greed, lust, envy, jealousy and many more, are in your brain 24/7 dictating your every move. These you think are your own thoughts. Think about this next statement. Who would give up consciousness if they knew the outcome would be a loss of control?

"There is so much more I want to tell you, but you can't bear it now. ¹³When the Spirit of truth comes, he will guide you into all truth. He will not speak on his own but will tell you what he has heard. He will tell you about the future. ¹⁴He will bring me glory by telling you whatever

he receives from me. ¹⁵All that belongs to the Father is mine; this is why I said, 'The Spirit will tell you whatever he receives from me.'"

(John 16:12-15).

THERE IS SO MUCH MORE!

In the above passage of Scripture, the LORD tells us *"there is so much more I want to tell you, but you can't bear it now!"* This expression dispels long-held religious notions that God desires to operate in eternal mystery; thus, we cannot expect to know all that can be known about God. Nothing could be further from the Truth. A God who goes through the meticulous effort of penning 66 books to reveal Himself to His creation is not a God who enjoys seeing His creation grapple in the dark helplessly trying to understand Him and His ways! It is clear from the statement made by Yeshua that God longs for His people to come into a consciousness of so much more! But Yeshua's desire to reveal Himself and the Father who sent Him did not end in frustration. To the contrary, His deep longing for His people to know more of His person and Kingdom ends in a glorious solution - the unveiling of the ministry of the precious Holy Spirit.

UNVEILING THE MINISTRY OF THE HOLY SPIRIT

The Lord Jesus Christ unveils the glorious ministry of the Holy Spirit around five main pillars that we will explore fully and how they relate to the subject of "consciousness." In chapter two, we also defined consciousness as follows: *"Consciousness is the awareness of the daily experience and interaction of your spirit and soul with the Holy Spirit."* True biblical consciousness, unlike consciousness as described by many in the New Age movement, involves the daily interaction between our spirit and soul with the Holy Spirit. Having established this fact, it follows that everything Yeshua ascribes to the ministry of the Holy Spirit has a direct impact on the subject of "consciousness." Thus, the power of consciousness lies in the fact that "consciousness" allows the believer to constantly engage the reality of the Living God in unbroken communion through the indwelling presence of the blessed Holy Spirit.

THE FIVE PILLARS OF THE MINISTRY OF THE HOLY SPIRIT

1. *When the Spirit of truth comes,*

2. *He will guide you into all truth.*

3. *He will not speak on His own but will tell you what He has heard.*

4. He will tell you about the future.

5. He will bring Me glory by telling you whatever He receives from Me.

Firstly, we will start by examining the expression, *"When the Spirit of truth comes"* and how it relates to the subject of consciousness. *When the Spirit of truth comes,* means that no human being can truly enter the domain of true biblical "consciousness" until he or she receives the "Spirit of Truth!" This completely eliminates every person in the so-called New Age movement who does not acknowledge Jesus Christ as Lord and Savior of the world. Acknowledging Christ as Lord and Savior is the first stepping-stone to receiving the "Spirit of Truth," who is the blessed Holy Spirit. Why does Yeshua call the Holy Spirit the "Spirit of Truth"? It is because the Scriptures in both the Old and New Testaments demonstrate that the Spirit of God is the supernatural search engine of the Godhead.

> *But it was to us that God revealed these things by his Spirit. For his Spirit searches out everything and shows us God's deep secrets. [11]No one can know a person's thoughts except that person's own spirit, and no one can know God's thoughts except God's own Spirit. [12]And we have received God's Spirit (not the world's spirit), so we can know the wonderful things God has freely given us*

> (1 Corinthians 2:10-12).

GOD'S SEARCH ENGINE

Before the world was mesmerized by the technological discovery of super search engines, such as Google, Bing or Yahoo, the Bible refers to the Holy Spirit as the master search engine in all of creation. There is nothing that is within the realms of truth and error that the Holy Spirit does not know of. The Scriptures declare that the Spirit searches all things, even the deep things related to the Godhead. This is why knowing the blessed Holy Spirit intimately is the holy grail of true "consciousness." Without this intimate knowledge of the Holy Spirit, how can we know if what we call "consciousness" is rooted in the "Truth or in error?" This is why many in the New Age movement who are sincerely passionate about the subject of "consciousness" end up worshipping their minds and ego in the name of "consciousness." They end up sitting on the thrones of their own hearts as God, which is the greatest deception of all. Such a take on "consciousness" makes them an easy prey for the devil who is roaming around like a roaring lion seeking persons whose souls he can devour. We can never truly know the "Truth" from a lie because "Truth is a Person" and only the Holy Spirit can effectively reveal this person - the Lord Jesus Christ who is the essence of the Truth.

Jesus saith unto him, I am the way, the truth, and the life: no man cometh unto the Father, but by me

(John 14:6, KJV).

WHO IS GUIDING YOU?

Secondly, Jesus uses the expression *"He will guide you into all truth."* This expression builds upon the first resolution that the Holy Spirit is the "Spirit of Truth"! This expression leaves no room for any other spirit guide for humans other than the blessed Holy Spirit. It is very common for many in the New Age movement to seek spirit guides that illuminate the pathway to higher levels of consciousness. In 1Chronicles 10:13, the Bible summarizes the death of King Saul as follows: *"So Saul died because he was unfaithful to the LORD. He failed to obey the LORD's command, and he even consulted a medium [14] instead of asking the LORD for guidance. So the LORD killed him and turned the kingdom over to David son of Jesse.*

This Scripture is very tragic when you consider the cradle of Saul's humble beginnings and how he sought the Lord at the inception of his kingship. But along the way, his perennial disobedience to God gave ample room to the demonic powers to rob him of "consciousness." He lost the minute-by-minute consciousness of the presence of God and began to seek other spirit guides (mediums), sealing his own destruction. The Holy Spirit is the only spirit-being on earth authorized by the Godhead to guide all spiritual seekers into higher levels of "Truth" that produce higher levels of true biblical "consciousness."

A FAITHFUL ADVOCATE

Thirdly, Yeshua uses the expression *"He will not speak on his own but will tell you what he has heard."* This expression adds another layer to the role the Holy Spirit plays in establishing true biblical consciousness. *"He will not speak on his own but will tell you what he has heard"* means that "consciousness" that is birthed by the Holy Spirit in the spirits of the redeemed of the LORD is a byproduct of the firey communion that exists eternally between the members of the Godhead. This means that one of the Holy Spirit's primary assignments is to bring humans into a place of intimate, minute-by-minute fellowship with the Godhead. The latter part of the expression *"...will tell you what he has heard"* means that the Holy Spirit does not have His own agenda that He wants to impose upon us other than what is on the mind of God. Life has taught me that you can always trust a person who has no agenda, because they are free from the pressure to manipulate you towards their hidden agenda. The Holy Spirit has no agenda of His own except to reveal Christ, the image of the invisible God in a human body. This is the reason the Holy Spirit is the only one who can bring people into "Christ-Consciousness!" The Holy Spirit is completely dedicated to revealing Christ and forming Him in His people everywhere!

STOP FEARING THE FUTURE

Fourthly, Jesus makes another very powerful statement about the blessed Holy Spirit, *"He will tell you about the future."* This statement ought to cheer every weary or troubled heart that is frightened by the prospects of a future unknown. Worrying about the future (tomorrow) is the primary source of stress in the lives of most men and women around the world. If we fail to elevate our consciousness concerning this vital area of human existence, our stress levels will only accelerate. Many Bible-believing believers are guilty of "idolizing the future" by making it more captivating than the precious minute-by-minute communion with the living God in the moment called "Now"!

But Yeshua shows us a sure way of escape from "worrying about the future" by declaring that the Holy Spirit will tell you about the future. For the longest time I used the expression the "Holy Spirit has been to your future," until the LORD corrected my erroneous proclamation. He said to me, "I have NOT been to the future I AM your future!" Furthermore, God is a God who created TIME but is not subject to it. TIME as a governing concept does not exist in the realms of eternity or timelessness. God has neither past nor future within Himself, because "future" implies a place on the timeline that you have never been before, and if you are God that is not possible. There is no place in TIME or in eternity where God has not already been.

While God has no measurable past or future, we as humans do. This is because man's existence and the outworking of God's eternal purposes for mankind transpire in a test tube called TIME! Since we live in a Time capsule that is constantly moving away from a "past point" to a "future point" on the timeline, it is easy to see why we are so obsessed with wanting to know the future (what lies ahead). Unfortunately, because of our diminished "consciousness," a very disempowering "fear consciousness" drives most of our thoughts about the future! Many so-called Christian homes are shuttering under the stressful weight of fretting about the future. But Jesus Christ informs us that one of the primary assignments of the Holy Spirit is to radically transform our "consciousness" towards the future that most people in our world consider elusive and fearsome. I am reminded of the word of the LORD to Jeremiah the prophet, , *"For I know the plans, I have for you," says the Lord. "They are plans for your welfare not for disaster, to give you a future and a hope" (Jeremiah 29:11).*

LIVING FOR GOD'S GLORY

Finally, the Lord Jesus Christ gives us the fifth pillar to the ministry of the Holy Spirit. He declares, *"He will bring me glory by telling you whatever he receives from me."* This statement defines the proper boundaries of true biblical consciousness. True biblical consciousness circumcises our hearts from our inherent propensity to get the credit for what God is doing in our lives instead of giving glory to God. As the Holy Spirit shifts our "consciousness," He will initiate in us a deep desire to give God glory for even the mundane things of life. We will suddenly begin to see the finger and footprints of God all over the canvas of creation. We will be thoroughly cleansed in our minds from believing in the garbage of evolution. We will see intelligent design in the tapestry of Creation, and we will bow down and worship in holy array He who lives forever and ever! It takes a higher level of consciousness to see God as being "all and in all!" Such is the true power of "consciousness!"

EATING FOOD OFFERED TO IDOLS

But if any man love God, the same is known of him. 4 As concerning the eating of those things that are offered in sacrifice unto idols, we know that an idol is nothing in the world, and that there is none other God but one. 5 For though they be that are called gods, whether in heaven or on earth, (as there be gods many, and lords many,) 6 But to us there is but one God, the Father, of whom are all things, and we in him; and one Lord Jesus Christ, by whom are all things and we by him. 7 Howbeit there is not in every man that knowledge: for some with conscience of the idol unto this hour eat it as a thing offered unto an idol; and there conscience being weak is defiled.

I Corinthians 8:3-7 (KJV)

Perhaps there is no passage of Scripture that clearly demonstrates the power of consciousness as the above passage of Scripture. The apostle Paul begins the Scriptural passage by making a very powerful statement. He declares that if any man loves God "the same is known of God." This statement means that if you truly love the Lord, your love for God will be registered in heaven and in the heart of God. The apostle then moves further to tackle a very sensitive subject that was affecting the church at Corinth. He addresses the issue of eating food offered in sacrifice to idols, "Was it okay or was it sinful?" I'm sure if I polled many Christians concerning their stand on this question I bet that the majority of Christians would say eating food offered to idols is demonic and sinful. But that's not what the great apostle to the church tells us in this passage. Paul makes it very clear that idols are "actually nothing in this world" because there is only one true God.

Most idols worshiped by men in different religions are actually created by men who then give their allegiance to these man-made gods. Paul declares that for this reason he has no problem eating food offered to idols. This is because in his "governing consciousness" the apostle knew that there is only one true God (El Elyon) and every idol is nothing but the creation of fallen men. But he goes further in his argument and says something that directly impacts the subject matter of this book, the subject of consciousness. He declares that even though he knew that I idols are nothing in this world because there is only one true God he would not eat food sacrificed to idols in the presence of another brother or sister in Christ whose consciousness towards eating food offered to idols is weak. In other words if you are eating food offered to idols in the presence of a brother or sister in Christ who truly believe it's demonic and sinful to do so, you are going to offend such a brother or sister in Christ if you eat the same. Such a brother or sister may not be able to go to sleep because in there mind they would be thinking that one of their brothers or sister in Christ is serving the devil because he or she is eating food offer to idols. Notwithstanding that idols are really nothing but creations of fallen man, who is searching for his long lost relationship with His maker. The main point behind this passage is to demonstrate the power of consciousness over the life of a child of God. The underlying issue in the above passage of scripture is not sin but consciousness. Paul's consciousness of who God was and who he was in Him was so high that eating food offered to idols was not a problem for him. Paul knowing that no human being can above their consciousness warns us to be careful not to offend other children of God whose revelation does not match up to ours.

LIFE APPLICATION SECTION

MEMORY VERSE

For all who are led by the Spirit of God are children of God. ¹⁵So you have not received a spirit that makes you fearful slaves. Instead, you received God's Spirit when he adopted you as his own children. Now we call him, "Abba, Father." ¹⁶For his Spirit joins with our spirit to affirm that we are God's children

(Romans 8:14-16).

1. What are the Five Pillars of the Ministry of the Holy Spirit?

2. Why is the Holy Spirit referred to as the "Spirit of Truth"?

Chapter Five
A FALLEN KING CALLED TIME

To everything there is a season, a time for every purpose under heaven:
² A time to be born, and a time to die; a time to plant, and a time to
pluck what is planted; ³ a time to kill, and a time to heal; a time to
break down, and a time to build up; ⁴ a time to weep, and a time to
laugh; a time to mourn, and a time to dance; ⁵ a time to cast away
stones, and a time to gather stones; a time to embrace, and a time to
refrain from embracing; ⁶ a time to gain, and a time to lose; a time to
keep, and a time to throw away; ⁷ a time to tear, and a time to sew; a
time to keep silence, and a time to speak; ⁸ a time to love, and a time to
hate; a time of war, and a time of peace

(Ecclesiastes 3:1-8, NKJV).

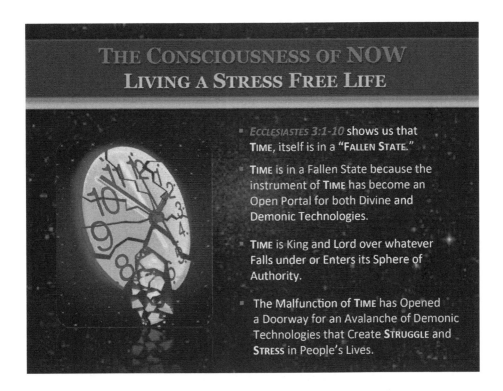

Unfortunately, when Adam and Eve (the first Kingdom Ambassadors) *fell*
from glory and dominion, the womb of TIME fell with them and morphed into
a terrible taskmaster. Before the Fall, the womb of TIME was under Adam's
dominion, but after the fall of Adam and Eve, all of mankind became servants

of Time. Since then, the world we live in is controlled and governed by a king called *Time*. *Time* has become so powerful in the world we live in, that it is now a universally accepted fact that *time is money*. The people of our planet exchange their time in order to get money. *Consequently, the king called Time now controls the financial resources of so many people including Citizens of the Kingdom of God.* In the lives of many followers of Christ, *Time* has such a mastery over them that many even struggle to find the time to spend with the Lord. This is why it is important for us to understand the hidden meaning behind the passage from the book of Ecclesiastes.

THE WOMB OF TIME

In the above passage of Scripture King Solomon shows us that the *womb of Time* is in a fallen state. He shows us that *Time* has deviated from its God intended purpose. To prove his point, Solomon gives us *a parade of contrasts*, which are all transpiring within the cylinder of TIME continuum. He says that there is *a time to kill, a time to heal, a time to hate, a time to love and so forth*. What is important to note here is that the *womb of Time in its fallen state is manifesting both divine and demonic technologies. Time,* which was only ordained to manifest the divine purposes of God, now makes allowances to bring forth the seed of the enemy. *Time* has become an open portal for both the divine and the demonic. It is clear from King Solomon's observation of time that there are two competing frequencies within the cylinder of TIME: *the frequency of heaven and the frequency of the demonic kingdom.* Since man lives within the cylinder of TIME, these opposing frequencies bombard him constantly. Mankind is sandwiched between these two opposing frequencies. Each new day presents us with opportunities to choose between these two opposing frequencies: whether to work with God or the demonic. This is why God told the children of Israel through the prophet Moses, "*I have set before you life and death, blessing and cursing; therefore choose life.*" If the Holy Spirit does not lead us, we will perpetually succumb to the demonic frequency within the cylinder of TIME, which easily appeals to our lower nature.

This perpetual mixing of divine and demonic frequencies within the *cylinder of TIME* creates endless opportunities for the people of our planet to either experience peace or devastation depending upon the frequency that is animating their nature. *The presence of demonic frequencies within the cylinder of TIME is the reason why life on earth is full of situations that increase and exacerbate people's stress levels.* This is why it is important for God's people to find a biblical response to the malfunctioning of Time, so that they can escape *the tyranny of fallen Time.* Man was never created to serve *Time* but *Time* was created to serve man. Man was created by God and for God's pleasure. This means that Man is only allowed to serve God and not *Time*. Serving *Time* instead of serving God is idolatry. Nature also teaches us this principle. We contemptuously call people who are serving "time" in correctional facilities "prisoners." Consequently, when *Time* disagrees with God or His Word, we must bring the dictates of *Time* under subjection to the cosmic authority of the Christ in us; bending *Time* in the direction of the "Will of God!"

BENDING THE CURVATURE OF TIME

One of the clearest biblical examples of this powerful truth is the story of Joshua and the children of Israel. The Bible tells us that there came a day when Joshua was fighting with the enemies of Israel for the right to the Promised Land. God was giving him great victory over his enemies but something was threatening to abruptly stop his momentum. "Time" was threatening to close the door on his victorious momentum. *Realizing this Joshua commanded "Time" to come to a standstill for twelve hours so he could finish God's work;* henceforth, demonstrating God's original intent for the relationship between Man and Time. *Time* must never dictate to a man filled with God's purpose whether he can finish the work of God or not. *To the contrary, man is to dictate to Time what he needs it to do so he can finish the work of God.* This is the reason why in Scripture the LORD has never accepted *Time* as a reasonable excuse for disobeying His call upon our lives. When Jeremiah told the Lord that he was too young to answer the call to become a prophet, the Lord completely disregarded his objection. This is because "age" is nothing but man's measurement of *Time*. Had the Lord accepted Jeremiah's excuse of being too young as a legitimate reason to be excused from doing the work of God; God would have in effect submitted Himself to His own creation. *Time* is a creation of God and God never submits Himself to His creation. This is why there is no human being who is too old or young to serve the Lord. Age is nothing but a dot on the timeline.

A KING CALLED TIME

Nevertheless in order to tip the scales and change the balance of power between us and *Time*, we need to come into a heightened state of the same kind of *Sonship-consciousness that the Lord Jesus Christ and Joshua exhibited when they were on earth.* When the Lord Jesus Christ finally showed up after the death and burial of Lazarus, both Mary and Martha told Him that had He been there three days prior, their brother would never have died. In other words, they were telling Yeshua that He was three days too late. What spirit do you think was speaking through the mouths of Mary and Martha? It is the demonic frequency that operates in *Time* that limits the power of God in people's lives based upon their false perception of *Time*. Mary and Martha were both loyal and Christ-loving disciples but internally they were more devoted to a king called *Time* than to the eternal King of Glory who was standing in front of them. This is the reason the Lord Jesus Christ stayed three more days after He was informed that Lazarus was deathly ill. He wanted to use this circumstance to deliver His disciples from serving the tyrant king called *Time.*

When the Lord was giving me the revelation on *the Consciousness of Now,* He asked me a very interesting question. The Holy Spirit asked me, *"What expression do you use to describe a person who was put in jail by the governing authorities?"* I said to the Lord that in America we say, *"They are doing time or serving time."* The Lord then proceeded to give me a revelation that affected me deeply. He said, *"Many of My people are also prisoners because a prisoner is by definition a person who is serving Time. When my people serve Time instead of serving Me, they become prisoners to Time and the demonic entities that operate within it."* This powerful revelation left me speechless and then induced repentance in my heart. I saw many areas of my life where I was also a prisoner of *Time.* But the only way for all of us to get paroled from serving *Time* is to enter into a new way of thinking or consciousness. We need to possess God's own consciousness towards *Time*

REDEEMING TIME

Redeeming the time, because the days are evil

(Ephesians 5:16, NKJV).

In the New Testament one of Christ's greatest apostles, Paul, also believed that "Time" is in a fallen state. This is because when mankind fell, everything that was under man's dominion fell with him into the same bondage of corruption. This is why the Apostle Paul uses the expression *"redeeming the time for the days are evil."* Scripture teaches us that you can only redeem something that is already in a fallen state. Christ came to redeem us because we are all in a fallen state. Consequently, if *Time* is being redeemed it follows that *Time* is also in a fallen state.

So the million-dollar question, or the elephant in the room, is this: *"How do you redeem Time?"* You can only redeem *Time* by walking in the Spirit and not following the dictates of *Time* continuum. Walking in the Spirit is one of the quickest ways to redeem *Time.* This is why the Apostle says in the book of Romans, *"As many as are led by the Spirit of God, they are sons of God."* Being led by the Spirit can save us many years of unnecessary toil and sweat that would otherwise have been our portion had the Spirit not led us.

Walk in wisdom toward them that are without, redeeming the time

(Colossians 4:6, NKJV).

Based upon the above passage of Scripture, another way that we redeem *Time* is by walking in the wisdom of God towards the people of this world.

Sometimes we can waste *Time* unnecessarily trying to reach the unreachable and argumentative. This is why Scripture declares that he who wins souls is wise. This means that the winning of souls requires the wisdom of God so we do not spend energy toiling in the soils of the heart of people who are not ready to respond to the Gospel of the Kingdom.

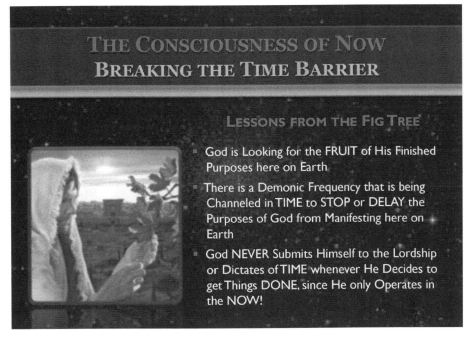

THE CONSCIOUSNESS OF NOW
BREAKING THE TIME BARRIER

LESSONS FROM THE FIG TREE

- God is Looking for the FRUIT of His Finished Purposes here on Earth
- There is a Demonic Frequency that is being Channeled in TIME to STOP or DELAY the Purposes of God from Manifesting here on Earth
- God NEVER Submits Himself to the Lordship or Dictates of TIME whenever He Decides to get Things DONE, since He only Operates in the NOW!

LESSONS FROM THE FIG TREE

And seeing a fig tree afar off having leaves, he came, if haply he might find any thing thereon: and when he came to it, he found nothing but leaves; for the time of figs was not yet

(Mark 11:13, KJV).

Perhaps there is no biblical story that clearly demonstrates the relationship between the Lord Jesus Christ and the fallen king called *Time* as the story of the fig tree. Perhaps the most important question that we must ask ourselves is, "Why did the Holy Spirit allow this story to make it into the canon of Scripture?" The Bible tells us that everything that Yeshua did while He was on earth, is not recorded in the Gospels. If everything Yeshua did while He was on the earth was recorded, there would not be enough books to record them all. Consequently, whatever the LORD allowed to enter the Gospels is of very high value.

We are told that one day the Lord Jesus Christ was on His way to Bethany when He came across a fig tree. What is interesting about this particular fig tree is that when Yeshua approached it for fruit, the Scriptures declare that it was not yet "time" for figs. It would seem that any reasonable man would simply shrug his shoulders and walk away from a fig tree whose time for fruit was not yet. But this is not what Christ did.

To the contrary, Yeshua ignored the fact that nature said that it was not "time" for the fig tree to bear fruit. Instead, He looked at its green leaves and desired "fruit" from the tree. Finding no fruit, Yeshua cursed the fig tree from its root system. The disciples found the Messiah's behavior towards the fig tree odd, to say the least. But on their way back, Peter screamed with bewilderment when he saw that the fig tree that Yeshua had cursed had dried up within twenty-four hours! In response, Yeshua tells them that they could also control nature if they had the "faith of God"!

Nevertheless, the million-dollar question is, "Why did Yeshua approach the fig tree when it was not yet "time" for it to bear fruit. The portals of divine revelation opened over me one day and what the Holy Spirit showed me had me shouting! The Holy Spirit showed me that there were three main reasons why Jesus did what He did.

First, the fig tree represents the children of the Kingdom who have been in the faith for a while, who have a form of godliness (the green leaves) while denying the true power of the gospel (the fruit). These men and women have allowed the things that have happened to them in *Time* to choke the "fruit" of the Word of God in their lives. They talk the talk but cannot walk the walk; ever learning but never coming into the knowledge of the truth. These people are in danger of losing their place of stewardship in the Kingdom.

Second, Yeshua approached the fig tree when *Time* said it was not supposed to bear fruit to show His disciples that they were not to accept the dictates of "Time and Space" over the revealed will of God. When God says our harvest is ready, we cannot allow *Time* to tell us otherwise. *Time* may say that it will take thirty years for us to pay off our mortgage; meanwhile the Spirit wants to pay it off in two years! If we do not know that *Time* is in a fallen state, we will easily accept the dictates of *Time*. Yeshua as God, was NOT going to subject Himself to the dictates of something that He created. In Joshua's day, *Time* was threatening to close the window on his victorious momentum over his enemies. But Joshua was not to be denied. He asked the LORD to hold the Sun and *Time* obeyed; it stopped moving for twelve hours! Glory to God!

And finally, Yeshua approached the fig tree out of its due season to show us that if we have the "faith of God" we can move "Time and Space" in our favor. He was showing us that having the "God-kind-of-faith" would deliver us from the tyranny of "Time and Space." He was showing us that with faith we can overturn natural law and change the course of human history. If we had the faith of God we could accelerate "Time" and invoke our harvest to get to us much earlier than previously anticipated!

Chapter Six

THE GEOMETRY OF ETERNITY AND TIME

That which hath been is now; and that which is to be hath already been; and God requireth that which is past.

(Ecc 3:11-15)

While it is true that "time" is in a fallen state it is also true that there yet remains a supernatural geometry between eternity and time that is beautiful to behold. This is why the revelation on the "consciousness of Now" is so important. This revelation will help us to profit from the supernatural alignment between eternity and time whenever God sovereignly intervenes in the affairs of men. For instance a bright Eastern Star that spoke of the supernatural alignment between God's eternal purposes and time continuum guided the magi from the East to where the baby Jesus was. The Eastern Star guided the Magi who brought the Lord Jesus Christ great gifts of honor to worship Him with when

He was born. The story of the Magi is a perfect example of the supernatural geometry that exists between eternity and time.

Now when Jesus was born in Bethlehem of Judaea in the days of Herod the king, behold, there came wise men from the east to Jerusalem, 2 Saying, Where is he that is born King of the Jews? for we have seen his star in the east, and are come to worship him.

Matthew 2:1-3 (KJV)

DANIEL'S INHERITANCE

The Jewish historian Josephus gives us a probable reason as to why the Magi appeared in Bethlehem to worship the King of kings with great gifts of honor. Josephus believes that the Magi came out of ancient Babylon in order to consummate Daniel's enduring legacy. Daniel was a very highly esteemed chief of the magicians in ancient Babylon, even though he was actually a prophet of the Most High God. His name was legendary in ancient Babylon. It is said that before Daniel died he pledged all the wealth that he had accumulated in Babylon to the coming Messiah of the Jewish people. It is believed that Daniel brought the Council of the Magi into a solemn oath. Daniel made the Magi pledge to take the wealth he had amassed in Babylon to the King of kings would be born in Bethlehem. This would make sense because Daniel never married while he was in Babylon, which means that he had no sons or daughters to pass on his inheritance. Being a prophet of God and having been shown the exact appearance of the Messiah within the timeline Daniel knew exactly what prophetic signs to look for within the "womb of TIME" in order to determine the exact time and birthplace of the Messiah. The above scenario is why the devil is very afraid of men and women who are like the sons of Issachar; who have an understanding of the "times" and what they ought to do.

*And **of the** children **of** Issachar, which were men that had **understanding of the times**, to know what Israel ought to do;*

1 Chronicles 12:32 (KJV)

MOMENTS OF KAIROS TERRIFY THE DEVIL

When Herod the king had heard these things, he was troubled, and all Jerusalem with him.4 And when he had gathered all the chief priests and scribes of the people together, he demanded of them where Christ should be born. 5 And they said unto him, In Bethlehem of Judaea: for thus it is written by the prophet, 6 And thou Bethlehem, in the land of Juda, art not the least among the princes of Juda: for out of thee shall come a Governor, that shall rule my people Israel. 7 Then Herod, when he had privily called the wise men, enquired of them diligently what time the star appeared. Matthew 2:1-7 (KJV)

There is a supernatural time in the spirit called "Kairos." In the Greek language the name for natural time is known as "Chronos." Chronos is where we get the word chronological. Chronos suggests time that flows in a sequential order, minute-by-minute, day-by-day, year by year and so forth. There is nothing supernatural about "Chronos," on the other hand "Kairos" is a supernatural time that is created on the timeline when eternity kisses time continuum. Whenever eternity kisses "Chronos" or intersects with the timeline a supernatural moment in God is created in which all things that happen in that "spot of time" carry the supernatural touch of God.

The appearance of the Magi in the palace of King Herod to announce the supernatural birth of the King of kings represents a time of "Kairos." It is a time in which God's eternal purposes intersect with time continuum and there is absolutely nothing the devil can do to stop the manifestation of God's predetermined purpose during these special times. But if we are not functioning in the "consciousness of now" it will be very difficult for us to discern when these supernatural times are upon us. The creation of these supernatural times of the God encounter within man's time zone is what I called the geometry of eternity and time.

When King Herod learnt through the Magi that the supernatural time for the birth of the promised Messiah had come upon them he was very terrified. He knew that no two kingdoms could coexist side by side. Unfortunately for King Herod what he did not understand is that the Messiah was a king of a much higher and spiritual kingdom. If he had known that the baby in swaddling clothes lying in a manger was the king of kings and creator of the universe, King Herod would have led his own entourage to worship the king of kings and his history as king would've been very different. Instead he is remembered for the massacre of thousands of innocent children in his failed attempt to kill the baby Jesus.

THE APOSTOLIC ALIGNMENT OF TIME

When they had heard the king, they departed; and, lo, the star, which they saw in the east, went before them, till it came and stood over where the young child was. 10 When they saw the star, they rejoiced with exceeding great joy. 11 And when they were come into the house, they saw the young child with Mary his mother, and fell down, and worshipped him: and when they had opened their treasures, they presented unto him gifts; gold, and frankincense and myrrh. 12 And being warned of God in a dream that they should not return to Herod, they departed into their own country another way.

Matthew 2:9-12 (KJV)

When the Magi arrived in Jerusalem loaded with treasures to worship the Messiah who had been born in Bethlehem there was an apostolic alignment of time. We will examine a couple of powerful apostolic factors that transpire when there is an apostolic alignment of time.

- The first thing we see when there is an apostolic alignment of time is that "nature" itself rises to cooperate with the fulfillment of our God given destiny. The star in this story represents nature lining itself with the Magi so that they could find their way to the king of kings. When there is an apostolic alignment of time it would seem that everything in creation is cooperating with us to make sure that we have all the resources we need to fulfill God's call upon our life. This is why the devil is terrified of men and women that walk with God coming into these powerful moments of "Kairos."

- The second thing we see when there is an apostolic alignment of time is that we come into a supernatural manifestation of the joy of the Lord in our life. Gone are the days of serving God without joy. The supernatural alignment of time affords us the luxury of serving God without striving.

- The third thing we see when there is an apostolic alignment of time is that we come into profitable divine relationships. Without much effort on our part the right people begin to enter our life and the wrong people begin to exit our life.

- The fourth thing that happens when there is an apostolic alignment of time is that we begin to come into a powerful place of material prosperity. The apostolic alignment of time repositions us into strategic positions of power and prosperity. The apostolic alignment of time repositioned the parents of the baby Jesus so that they were at the right time and place for the arrival of the Magi. When the Magi arrived they brought the baby Jesus lots of money that enabled his parents to afford him a good life.

- The fifth thing that happens when there is an apostolic climate of time is that we begin to receive powerful prophetic dreams and visions from the Lord. The supernatural intervention of God becomes very real during these times. The Lord appeared to the Magi in a dream and told them not to go back to king Herod because he meant the child harm.

DECLARING THE END FROM THE BEGINNING

*Declaring the end from the beginning, and from **ancient times** the things that are not yet done, saying, My counsel shall stand, and I will do all my pleasure:*

Isaiah 46:10 (KJV)

They are very few scriptures in the Bible that clearly demonstrate the supernatural relationship between eternity and time like the above passage of scripture from the book of Isaiah. The expression *"declaring the end from the beginning"* implies that God's invisible hand is supernaturally manipulating what's happening within our linear world using His foreknowledge. God's foreknowledge is truly what creates this special relationship between eternity and time. God's foreknowledge is His inert ability to know something before it happens in time. This also means that when anything breaks down in "time" God is able to fix it and realign it once more with His eternal purposes.

Understanding this aspect of divinity is going to deliver us from thinking that our past can disqualify us from being used by God. Unfortunately many of God's children are laboring under this false notion that their past indiscretions are so egregious as to completely negate their God given destiny. Nothing could be further from the truth. In His foreknowledge God foresaw the fact that Adam and Eve would sin against Him so He prepared Christ as the lamb slain from before the foundation of the world; such is the geometry of eternity and time. Whenever men fall short, God orchestrates the supernatural intersection of eternity and time until a supernatural portal opens up within our realm so as to fix what's broken in our world.

TIME APPOINTED BY THE FATHER

Now I say, That the heir, as long as he is a child, differeth nothing from a servant, though he be lord of all;2 But is under tutors and governors until the time appointed of the father.3 Even so we, when we were children, were in bondage under the elements of the world:4 But when the fulness of the time was come, God sent forth his Son, made of a woman, made under the law,5 To redeem them that were under the law, that we might receive the adoption of sons.

Galatians 4:1-5 (KJV)

One of the many reasons why there is a supernatural geometry between eternity and time is because they are *"times appointed by the heavenly Father"* that must be manifested here on earth before the consummation of the ages in Christ Jesus. One of the times appointed by the heavenly father is a "set time" that allows every child of God who reaches a certain level of spiritual maturity to enter into his or her full inheritance in Christ Jesus! Before our spiritual maturity triggers this supernatural set time appointed by the heavenly Father the Bible tells us that we are no different from children who are held in bondage by the elements of this world.

The supernatural birth of Jesus Christ marked the tipping point in the curvature of history. Yeshua was born in what the Apostle Paul calls "the fullness of times;" a supernatural set time appointed by the Father! After the fall of man in the Garden of Eden, God prophesied to the serpent about the supernatural birth of a "violent seed of the woman" that would crush the head of the serpent. Throughout the ages the devil and his coalition of fallen angels have tried unsuccessfully to abort the entrance of the Messiah into our time driven world. The reason the devil failed miserably is because there is no demonic entity that can overturn the power of "times appointed by the heavenly Father!" Developing the "Consciousness of Now" will enable us to discern when we have stepped into these "set times" appointed by the Father!

LIFE APPLICATION SECTION

MEMORY VERSE

Behold, I am with you and will keep you wherever you go, and will bring you back to this land; for I will not leave you until I have done what I have spoken to you." **16** *Then Jacob awoke from his sleep and said, "Surely the Lord is in this place, and I did not know it."*

Genesis 28:10-16 (NKJV)

1. What happens when there is an apostolic alignment of Time?

2. How did the Magi know where to find the baby Jesus?

Chapter Seven

IDOLIZING THE PAST AND FUTURE

And the whole congregation of the children of Israel murmured against Moses and Aaron in the wilderness: ³And the children of Israel said unto them, Would to God we had died by the hand of the Lord in the land of Egypt, when we sat by the flesh pots, and when we did eat bread to the full; for ye have brought us forth into this wilderness, to kill this whole assembly with hunger. ⁴Then said the Lord unto Moses, Behold, I will rain bread from heaven for you; and the people shall go out and gather a certain rate every day, that I may prove them, whether they will walk in my law, or no

(Exodus 16:2-4, KJV).

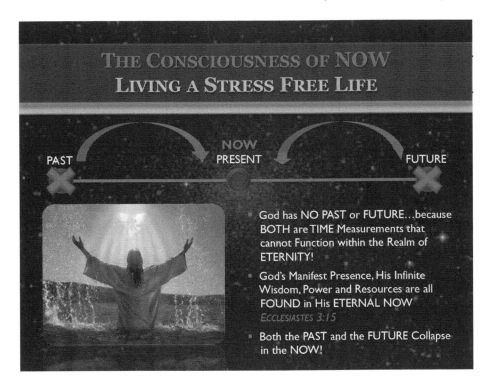

THE CONSCIOUSNESS OF NOW
LIVING A STRESS FREE LIFE

PAST   NOW   FUTURE
              PRESENT

God has NO PAST or FUTURE...because BOTH are TIME Measurements that cannot Function within the Realm of ETERNITY!

- God's Manifest Presence, His Infinite Wisdom, Power and Resources are all FOUND in His ETERNAL NOW *ECCLESIASTES 3:15*

- Both the PAST and the FUTURE Collapse in the NOW!

STUCK IN THE PAST

In the Geometry of *Time* continuum, the only point on the timeline that guarantees us the everlasting presence and influence of God is the moment called "NOW" Yet, the past continues to exert so much influence over the consciousness of so many people of faith. In the above passage of Scripture, the Bible tells us of the story of the children of Israel. These men and women had experienced tremendous sufferings at the hands of the Egyptians. Responding to their cry for deliverance and God's everlasting covenant with Abraham, the Lord raised a man named Moses, to bring deliverance to the children of Israel. God supernaturally delivered the children of Israel from Egyptian oppression by performing unparalleled signs and wonders to such an extent that they saw the armies of their oppressors drown into the bottom of the sea under a supernatural act of God. You would think that such a supernatural act would be enough antidote to deliver them from the tyranny of the past and convince them of the reality of the living God. But alas, such was not the case. The past still had great dominion over their collective consciousness. As such, at the least sign of trouble, the people began to bow down their knees to the God of the past. They challenged the leadership of Moses and admonished him for taking them out of Egypt, saying in effect that the past life of bondage was much better than walking with God in the "NOW"! This is why God wants His people to be delivered from the demonic consciousness that would seek to make them prisoners to their past. We have a daily invitation to have unbroken fellowship with the God of the "NOW" through the power of the Holy Spirit.

When the Lord sent Moses to the people of Israel to deliver them from the bondage that their Egyptian taskmasters had placed on them, the Lord made it very clear through Moses that He was taking them to a land full of milk and honey. To this end, God sent ten plagues to wrestle His people out of the hands of the Egyptians. But what Moses did not count on was how deeply rooted the past was in their consciousness. At every sign of trouble on their journey towards their full inheritance in Christ, the people would return to Egypt in their heart regardless of how much they had suffered under their Egyptian lords. This constant idolizing of the past in the hearts of the children of Israel was very frustrating to Moses. Moses thought the mighty deliverance at the hands of the Lord would have been enough to compel the children of Israel to change their consciousness. But to his great dismay, the past proved to be a great obstacle in their forward advancement towards the Promised Land.

ROBBED OF THEIR INHERITANCE

When your fathers tempted me, proved me, and saw my works forty years. ¹⁰Wherefore I was grieved with that generation, and said, They do always err in their heart; and they have not known my ways. ¹¹So I swore in my wrath, They shall not enter into my rest

(Hebrews 4:9-11, KJV).

Fast forward in the Bible to the book of Hebrews. The writer tells us of the tragic end of the people of Israel who idolized the past. The book of Hebrews tells us that the consciousness of the past robbed them of their true inheritance in Christ. Instead of entering the rest that comes from living in the center of His will, they were cut off from entering because they kept worshipping the past. Unfortunately for them, God is not a God of the past; He is the God of the "Now." The only thing that mattered to God was not what they had been through but what He was calling them into in the moment called "Now." God was calling them into the fellowship of the "Now" but they kept holding hostage the new and intimate relationship that God was offering them to events that happened to them in the past. It was quite clear that God, in His supernatural power, had taken them out of Egypt but they refused to allow Him to take Egypt out of their minds. We, too, must be careful to work tenaciously on changing our consciousness. Living in the past only strengthens demonic technologies against us. The only being who is excited at the prospect of us living in the past is the devil. This is because he is a master of the art of using the past against us. This is why the subject of this book, "The Consciousness of Now," is critical to living a victorious life in Christ Jesus in the last days. We must remember that the "Past" is already in the "Tomb." The best we can do with the past is to give it to God as our reasonable sacrifice.

THE IN-CHRIST FACTOR

Therefore if any man be in Christ, he is a new creature: old things are passed away; behold, all things are become new

(2 Corinthians 5:17, KJV).

In this passage of Scripture, the Apostle Paul demonstrates to us the abiding consciousness of our regenerated spirit. It is a consciousness completely free from the tyranny of the past. According to this passage, we are told that God completely annihilates the power of the past over the "New Creation" and makes all things new. Henceforth, the foundational consciousness of the New Creation is a consciousness which does not beat itself down over the failures and iniquities of the past. The expression, *"old things have passed away"* suggests that in the "New Creation" the Lord strips the past of its measure of rule.

In the timeline, the past has a very real and powerful measure of rule. It is the point in the timeline that reminds us of everything that we have ever done, good or bad. The devil loves using this point in our timeline to weigh us down with memories of past failures or indiscretions. But the "Past" can only exert its measure of rule over us if we fail to escape the tyranny of *Time* continuum. Since Christ is in God, God is also in Christ, and God exists eternally in the "Now;" we can conclude that the in-Christ factor that comes with our rebirth is very powerful for breaking free from the tyranny of the past.

TAKE NO THOUGHT

*Therefore I say unto you, Take no thought for your life, what ye shall eat, or what ye shall drink; nor yet for your body, what ye shall put on. Is not the life more than meat, and the body than raiment? *[26]*Behold the fowls of the air: for they sow not, neither do they reap, nor gather into barns; yet your heavenly Father feedeth them. Are ye not much better than they? *[27]*Which of you by taking thought can add one cubit unto his stature? *[28]*And why take ye thought for raiment? Consider the lilies of the field, how they grow; they toil not, neither do they spin: *[29]*And yet I say unto you, That even Solomon in all his glory was not arrayed like one of these. *[30]*Wherefore, if God so clothe the grass of the field, which to day is, and to morrow is cast into the oven, shall he not much more clothe you, O ye of little faith? *[31]*Therefore take no thought, saying, What shall we eat? or, What shall we drink? or, Wherewithal shall we be clothed? *[32]*(For after all these things do the Gentiles seek:) for your heavenly Father knoweth that ye have need of all these things. *[33]*But seek ye first the kingdom of God, and his righteousness; and all these things shall be added unto you. *[34]*Take therefore no thought for the morrow: for the morrow shall take thought for the things of itself. Sufficient unto the day is the evil thereof*

(Matthew 6:25-34, KJV).

While the children of Israel could not enter the Promised Land because they idolized the past, many born-again believers are just as guilty, if not more so, of idolizing the "Future." The "Future" like the past is a time measurement within the cylinder of *Time. To stress and worry over the future is to bow our knees at the altar of Time.* The Lord Jesus Christ introduces a very revolutionary concept that would have been impossible to believe had this concept not come out of the mouth of the Lord Himself. For what He is suggesting would seem to be humanly impossible. The Lord introduces this revolutionary concept with these words, *"take no thought for tomorrow."* The phrase, "Take no thought" is another way of telling us never to entertain worries about the future and yet, worrying about the future seems to be a subject our fallen nature has mastered very well. It would seem to me that everyone that I know is worried about his or her future. They are doing the very thing Yeshua said not to do which is worry about the future. Why would the Lord give us such impractical advice unless He knew that it is possible to exchange our worry-driven consciousness with a consciousness that is completely at rest with God's provision? We will now examine the areas Jesus Christ inferred are affected by this worry-free consciousness.

1. Our life

2. What we shall eat

3. What we shall drink

4. What we shall wear

5. The condition of our body

Jesus addresses what I call the "Five Pillars of Provision." These five areas cover the most important aspects of our lives here on earth. The expression, "take no thought for your life," addresses one of the most basic of human concerns – *the quality of life we expect to have while we are here on Earth.* Many people on our planet are constantly stressing over the quality of their life here on Earth. This is because we have an in-built God-given right that drives us towards the pursuit of happiness. Therefore, what Jesus is inferring is not designed to belittle these most basic human needs, but it is to say that God in His foreknowledge has already taken care of these important needs. This would explain why the Lord Jesus declared in the book of John that He came so we can have life in abundance. If the Lord has made provision for His people to have life in abundance, it makes sense why He would admonish us to not take thought of our life. He took care of the quality of our life when He hung on the Cross and said, "It is finished."

PUTTING FOOD ON THE TABLE

Yeshua goes a step further and admonishes us not to take thought of what we shall eat or drink. This statement does not in anyway suggest that the Lord does not want us to work for our provision. He is essentially admonishing us never to question His provision as though we were in doubt concerning its authenticity. In a worry and stress-driven culture such as ours, the Lord's admonition falls on deaf ears. We live in a culture that worships food as evidenced by the rise in obesity levels around the world. Telling a culture that is obsessed with eating and drinking not to worry about these issues truly requires a whole new level of consciousness. But this is exactly what the Lord Jesus Christ instructed us to do. Unless we enter into the same domain of Sonship-consciousness that Christ was operating in while He was on earth we will continue fretting about tomorrow.

Coincidentally, it is this same unbridled passion for food that led to the catastrophic fall of Adam and Eve in the glorious Garden of abundance. Since then, mankind's obsession with food has only escalated. Murders are committed every second around the world for a pound of food. But Christ's solution to this age-old problem remains undauntedly, "worry not about what you shall eat." When this prevailing Christ-consciousness envelops the mind of any child of God, it begins to rain provision in the life of the child of God so exercised.

WHAT SHALL I WEAR?

The Lord Jesus Christ goes even a step further and touches one of the most sensitive subjects concerning our existence – *what we shall wear*. He admonishes us not to worry or stress about what we shall wear. In a culture where outward looks and appearances are everything, Yeshua's admonition flies against our cultural trends. I know of women who will run up a credit card just to keep up with the latest fashions. This is because they are very worried of how other people view them on the basis of the clothes they wear. For such men and women, abiding by the Lord's admonition will surely require a new and higher level of consciousness. A close inspection of most people's wardrobes will reveal the fact that their wardrobes are cluttered with clothes they no longer wear but are afraid to let go of.

HOW DO I LOOK?

The Lord's final admonition in the text deals with another phenomenon in our culture – the physical condition of our body. While I agree that it is important for us to take care of our bodies, our culture's obsession with the physical appearance of the body borders on hardcore idolatry. There are women and men who are failing to walk out their spiritual destiny because they hate their physical appearance. They have bought into the lie that the condition of the body makes the person. There are women who are on self-imposed hunger strikes just to look petite and beautiful. I am reminded of the story of a famous model from Sweden who died of malnutrition in the name of looking beautiful.

The reality is that many of us, physically speaking, will never look like the iconic cover girl on most beauty magazines. What is of note is that many of these iconic cover girls on most beauty magazines have had their appearance altered by sophisticated computer technology. So if we base our self-worth on these unrealistic views of reality, we will open the door to lots and lots of stress. In the

Scriptures, beauty always begins from the inside out. We cannot base our true value on the basis of the shape and size of our body. This is why most people who try to lose weight in order to look beautiful never succeed. This is because they put undue pressure on themselves to thin down in order to love themselves.

Unfortunately, the stress created by such a warped sense of value only creates more stress within the anatomy of the body. Consequently, many end up gaining weight instead of losing weight. For some this warped view of self-worth has caused them to fall in such a pit of despair that they end up committing suicide because their body did not measure up to what they thought society expects them to be. In order to abide by the Lord's admonition not to worry about the body, many people will have to come into a higher level of consciousness.

LESSONS ON DIVINE PROVISION FROM NATURE

Behold the fowls of the air: for they sow not, neither do they reap, nor gather into barns; yet your heavenly Father feedeth them. Are ye not much better than they? [27]*Which of you by taking thought can add one cubit unto his stature?* [28]*And why take ye thought for raiment? Consider the lilies of the field, how they grow; they toil not, neither do they spin:*

(Matthew 6:26-28, KJV).

Finally, hoping to deal a deathblow to our stress-driven culture, the Lord Jesus shifts our attention to the immutable evidence of God's provision as evidenced in nature. Under this scenario, the Lord draws our attention to the fowls of the air and the lilies of the field. Concerning the fowls of the air, the Lord makes a very interesting observation. He demonstrates to us that the fowls of the air do not have the privilege of exercising the *"Law of sowing and reaping"* Yet, they never ever go without. Jesus said that the heavenly Father feeds them constantly. Then He shifts His argument to the lilies of the field. Yeshua notes that these beautiful flowers grow without toiling or spinning. These beautiful flowers are a prophetic picture of a life that is flourishing in the presence of God, without stress. Jesus is admonishing us to emulate these flowers. He is using these flowers to show us that there is a consciousness we can come into that will allow us to grow spiritually, emotionally and financially in the presence of God without stress.

He surmises His argument by asking a question that is known as a hyperbole. He asks us the question, *"Are you not more important to the heavenly Father than the fowls of the air or lilies of the field?"* The answer is an obvious "Yes." This being the case, worrying or stressing about our daily provision is a clear indication that we lack the kind of consciousness that the Lord is alluding to in this passage of Scripture. We are truly more valuable than the birds of the air and the Lilies of the field.

LIFE APPLICATION SECTION

Memory Verse

And the whole congregation of the children of Israel murmured against Moses and Aaron in the wilderness: ³And the children of Israel said unto them, Would to God we had died by the hand of the Lord in the land of Egypt, when we sat by the flesh pots, and when we did eat bread to the full; for ye have brought us forth into this wilderness, to kill this whole assembly with hunger. ⁴Then said the Lord unto Moses, Behold, I will rain bread from heaven for you; and the people shall go out and gather a certain rate every day, that I may prove them, whether they will walk in my law, or no (Exodus 16:2-4, KJV).

1. What is worshipping the Past?

2. What are the five pillars of divine provision?

Chapter Eight

THE CONSCIOUSNESS OF NOW

*He hath made every thing **beautiful in his time**: also he hath set the world in their heart, so that no man can find out the work that God maketh from the beginning to the end.*

Ecclesiastes 3:11 (KJV)

*He has made everything beautiful in its time. He also has **planted eternity in men's hearts** and minds [a divinely implanted sense of a purpose working through the ages which nothing under the sun but God alone can satisfy], yet so that men cannot find out what God has done from the beginning to the end.*

Ecclesiastes 3:11 (AMP)

We have already stated the fact that God created man to relate to "Consciousness." No consciousness is as critical to man's ability to live in dominion as the consciousness that he brings to his dealings with "Time continuum." We have already discussed the fact that TIME as we know it is in a fallen state. The "womb of TIME" was breached and compromised by the sin of Adam and Eve in the Garden of Eden. Since then the *womb of TIME* has given birth to both divine and demonic technologies, placing mankind in a perpetual fight between good and evil. This daily struggle by men and women who are trapped in "TIME" can produce a stress driven life unless we radically transform our "consciousness."

ESCAPING THE WORLD OF STRESS

In the above passage of Scripture, the Holy Spirit gives us an escape valve out of the stress driven culture that defines much of our world. It's an ancient pathway out of the daily grind that defines much of life today. King Solomon, the wisest and richest man who has ever lived, under the inspiration of the Holy Spirit informs us that God has made everything beautiful in "His time." He goes further and defines what God's TIME really is. We quickly discover that

67

"eternity" is God's TIME. God's TIME is timelessness, *time beyond time.* The preacher of righteousness tells us that God in His eternal genius has planted eternity in the hearts of men. *This planting of eternity in the hearts of men is the divinely embedded sense of eternal destiny within the hearts of man.* This seed of eternity in the hearts of men is the reason why men are so obsessed with questions about immortality. This seed of eternity in the heart of man is the reason why the "consciousness" of men all over the world, even those who ascribe to religions that do not acknowledge Christ as Lord, still grapple with nagging questions about the afterlife. Whether men or women know it or not, their spirit is in constant pursuit of a life that is free of the restraints of TIME and space. But since God has planted eternity in our hearts, we do not have to die in order to break free from the tyranny of TIME and space.

HE HAS MADE EVERYTHING BEAUTIFUL IN HIS TIME!

It's the object of this writing to bring you into God's time, so you can begin to experience the glory of eternity in the "Now!" In the above passage of Scripture, King Solomon tells us that *God has made everything beautiful in His TIME.* The expression "He has made everything beautiful in His TIME" does not mean that everything that happens in life is beautiful. Yeshua already told us *"in this world you shall have trouble but be of good cheer for I have overcome the world!"* As we have already stated, the womb of TIME is compromised enough to produce the works of the enemy in the lives of people. This means that bad things can happen to godly people because their life does intersect with the lives of evil men and women. But what the Scripture is telling us here is that if *we discern God's TIME and bring those bad experiences into His "TIME," God is able to make them beautiful!*

If discerning God's TIME is the key to transforming the bad and ugly experiences in our lives into something beautiful, then we must do all that we can to enter His TIME! So how then do we discover His TIME? The answer to this very important question lies at the heart of this entire book. My search for this answer is what led me to discover the revelation of the *"Consciousness of Now: a consciousness that is guaranteed to deliver anyone who embraces it from the tyranny of TIME and space."*

THE POWER OF THE NOW!

That which hath been is now; and that which is to be hath already been; and God requireth that which is past.

Ecclesiastes 3:15 (KJV)

In the above passage of Scripture, King Solomon makes a statement that on the surface seems redundant and yet he is actually giving us the *key to living a stress-free life.* King Solomon tells us that, *what has been* (Past) is <u>NOW</u> and that *which shall be* (Future) has *already been.* To help you grasp the power of what the Holy Spirit is unveiling through King Solomon, it is needful that you look at the following diagrams.

In geometry we live in what is known as a linear world, which is always represented by a line. In a linear world, the line is made up of three important indexes by which we measure TIME continuum. We will call the first point in the line "P1" which will represent the PAST, then we will call the middle point "P2" which represents the "PRESENT or NOW" and we will label the final index on the line "F1" representing the "FUTURE." Using this linear diagram, we can see that we live in a TIME driven world that is constantly moving between past, present and future. The PAST is that which we are coming from and the FUTURE is that which we hope to attain.

TIME SHALL NOT HAVE DOMINION OVER YOU!

The Holy Spirit told me that in a linear world these three "Time" measurements past, present and future have *a definitive measure of rule* within the timeline. This means that the PAST has *a defining measure of rule over those who are trapped in and by it.* The FUTURE also has a *defining measure of rule over the consciousness of those who are obsessed with it.* Similarly, the PRESENT or what I call the "NOW" also has *a very defining influence on the consciousness of men and women who are defined by it.* But how does understanding the "measure of rule" exerted by all of these time measurements relate to the question of how we can live a stress free life in this chaotic world? I am glad you asked me. I will show you what the Holy Spirit shared with me.

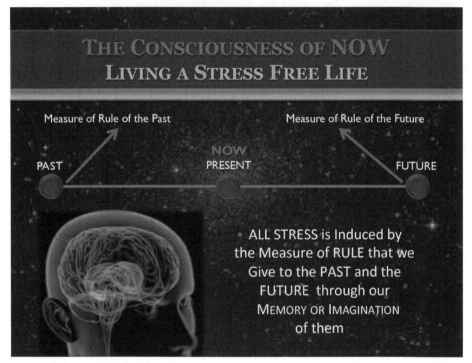

THE CONSCIOUSNESS OF NOW
LIVING A STRESS FREE LIFE

Measure of Rule of the Past — Measure of Rule of the Future

PAST — NOW PRESENT — FUTURE

ALL STRESS is Induced by the Measure of RULE that we Give to the PAST and the FUTURE through our MEMORY OR IMAGINATION of them

The Holy Spirit told me that any kind of stress that people experience is generated by only two of the three TIME measurements we have stated above. These two TIME measurements being the PAST and FUTURE. The PAST projects stress into our present by our memory of it. My dear spiritual mother and brain scientist, Dr. Aiko Hormann, once told me that the brain has no way of distinguishing between fantasy and reality. This is why man's 3-brains (the head, heart and gut brains) will release the same chemical responses in a man made simulation that mirrors an actual live event. In either case, the brain will release the exact same chemical responses into the body without any prejudice between an actual event and an imagined one. This behavior of the brain quickly unmasks why the PAST has so much power over people's consciousness. The world we live in is full of men and women who could be functioning at the apex of their God given capacity except for their memories of PAST events that stops them right in their tracks. I know men and women who were sexually molested when they were young who are still defined completely by this one tragic event. These people don't really have a future they just have a longer yesterday. Each time they try to move forward into the destiny that God has for them, the devil who also understands the mechanics of the brain is quick to trigger their memory of this one tragic event. Once the enemy triggers this unhealed memory the resolve of these men and women to move forward into their God given destiny collapses like a house of cards at the altar of this painful memory. Whether these men or women know it or not, they are actually *"trapped in a TIME warp"* that imprisons them to a life of endless pain, fear and ultimately defeat.

THE TYRANNY OF THE PAST

*But he knows not that the shades of the dead are there [specters haunting the scene of **past** transgressions], and that her invited guests are [already sunk] in the depths of Sheol (the lower world, Hades, the place of the dead).*

Proverbs 9:18 (AMP)

The above example is just one of the many real life situations that we could allude to. But what is of note here is that the kingdom that all of these men and women are trapped in is a kingdom where the PAST is "king." The kingdom where the PAST is king has millions of citizens who bow their knees daily at the altar of PAST events that they have failed to surrender to God. The Holy Spirit showed me how the memory of many of these tragic and painful PAST events can create a lot of stress in the lives of people who are trapped in this TIME warp. Since the PAST is just one of the measurements on the timeline, it follows that those who fail to get over their PAST are actually "serving TIME."

In the United States of America when a person is sent to prison, they are described as "serving or doing time." *By this definition, a prisoner is a person whose freedom has been taken away so they can "serve TIME" behind bars.* The Holy Spirit dropped an explosive revelation in my spirit that I had not considered before. He said to me that the body of Christ is also full of "spiritual prisoners" who are "serving or doing TIME" behind the bars of certain PAST events that they have failed to surrender completely to Jesus Christ. Mankind was never created to *serve TIME*, for that's what prisoners do. We were created to serve God, while "TIME" was created by God to "serve us!" But the tragic fall of Adam and Eve from "Consciousness" and from their God given place of dominion reversed "TIME's" God ordained role towards all mankind. Consequently, it behooves us to enter into a *higher level of consciousness* to be rescued from living in the kingdom where "Past" is king. We are called to live in a "Kingdom" where Christ is King!

WORSHIPPING THE FUTURE

I know that, whatsoever God doeth, it shall be forever: nothing can be put to it, nor any thing taken from it: and God doeth it, that men should fear before him. 15 That which hath been is now; and that which is to be hath already been; and God requireth that which is past.

Ecclesiastes 3:14-15 (KJV)

"So don't worry about tomorrow, for tomorrow will bring its own worries. Today's trouble is enough for today.

Matthew 6:34

By the grace of God I have had the distinct privilege of travelling to three continents. While the language, culture and customs of some of the nations I have been to are different from each other, there was a very common thread that bonded all these people groups. I observed this common bond with great interest. This common thread meanders into a "Universal consciousness." This universal consciousness is this undying obsession with the "future." While there is undoubtedly millions of citizens in the kingdom where "Past" is king, they are many more royal citizens in the kingdom where "Future" is king.

"You are an Idol worshipper, the Spirit declared!" I was deeply puzzled and got my feelings hurt. I really thought I was doing great in my relationship with the LORD until the Holy Spirit shattered any elusions to the contrary. "Oh Me!" I protested. I certainly did not see my self as an idol worshipper but the words of the Holy Spirit left no room for arguing the merits of my case. It was not a question the Spirit was posing, it was a statement of fact He was making. *"How can I be an idol worshipper, when I gave up idols to serve the Lord Jesus Christ?"* I asked myself in an effort to sooth my wounded spiritual pride. I did not have to wait long for the answer.

"You and most of my children around the world are Idol worshippers. You worship the *Future!* Anytime a child of God is more worried about what the future will bring to such an extent that they fail to enjoy the *'Presence of God in the Now;'* they are worshipping the future." Suddenly I saw it! The revelation flooded my spirit like the breaking of a flooding dam. My wounded pride forgotten, a spirit of repentance suddenly overtook me. Like someone watching a screenplay, I saw the many moments in my life that I have bowed my knees to a "god" called the future!

"So don't worry about tomorrow, for tomorrow will bring its own worries. Today's trouble is enough for today. Matthew 6:34

Many times in my life I have been so obsessed with worrying about the future that I couldn't enjoy the precious presence of God that was readily available to me in the moment called "Now!" I also noticed that the times I spent fretting about the future were also the times I was the most miserable. I was not only miserable but I made those around me miserable. In most cases my fretting about the future caused me to be edgy and shot at the mouth. In my warped thinking I felt justified to wallow in my misery because after all how could I not be, when my future was so uncertain? It did not take long before my fretting about the future turned into "stress and more stress!"

In the passage from the sixth chapter of Matthew, Yeshua is proposing a "consciousness" that is very foreign to our stress driven culture. He admonishes us *not to worry about tomorrow* and then goes on to tell us why. *"Today's trouble is enough for today!"* What Yeshua is proposing here would be laughable if He was not God! Being that He was God and came from God what He is proposing merits a thorough and forensic investigation. But how can we not worry about tomorrow, when that's what we humans are very good at?

Many of us have a PHD in worrying about tomorrow. But why is this the case? The Holy Spirit gave me the answer to this ageless problem of man. *"The reason most men worship the future is because they are not convinced that God has already secured the future for those who believe!"* This revelation sent streams of power throughout my entire being. The Holy Spirit proceeded to ask me a question that shook the very core of my being. *"Francis, how can the future that you are so worried about be anymore powerful than the presence of God that is readily available to you, in the Now?"* I knew that an idol is anything that has more power over our consciousness than the God Almighty! It began to dawn on me, how men became idol worshippers- worshipping the god of a future unknown. It suddenly dawned on me that "God" is my "Future!"

THE CONSCIOUSNESS OF NOW
LIVING A STRESS FREE LIFE

PAST — NOW PRESENT — FUTURE

- God has NO PAST or FUTURE...because BOTH are TIME Measurements that cannot Function within the Realm of ETERNITY!
- God's Manifest Presence, His Infinite Wisdom, Power and Resources are all FOUND in His ETERNAL NOW *ECCLESIASTES 3:15*
- Both the PAST and the FUTURE Collapse in the NOW!

GOD IS MY FUTURE!

Lord, you alone are my inheritance, my cup of blessing. You guard all that is mine. 6 The land you have given me is a pleasant land. What a wonderful inheritance!

Psalms 16:5-6

It suddenly dawned on me that if I walked into a future, in which I had all the provisions this world can offer but a future void of God's presence I would be very miserable! I suddenly had an idea of what hell must be like. Hell is not fearsome because of the endless torments it contains that are portrayed in most storybooks; it's the complete absence of the presence of God that is most fearsome. Hell with its endless torments would be most bearable if God's presence availed itself to it. But alas this is what truly makes hell, "hell" it's a timeless abode without God! Hell is a forbidding future without God. As this powerful revelation arrested my consciousness, I felt the idolatry of worshipping the future, begin to crumble under the weight of this awesome revelation. As I let go of worshipping the future, the stress that constantly overshadowed me began to dissipate. Peace like a mighty river began to wash over me.

LIVING IN THE NOW!

That which hath been is now; and that which is to be hath already been; and God requireth that which is past. (Ecc 3:15) KJV

After it became clear that any obsession with either the past or future was hardcore idolatry, I knew that I had a very important decision to make. How was I to live my life going forward in the face of this overwhelming revelation? Was I going to continue to allow myself to be a "Prisoner of TIME?" My answer was swift and resolute! I would live neither in the PAST nor in the FUTURE but in the Now! It became clear to me that the only point in the timeline where I would always encounter God's presence is in the moment called, Now!

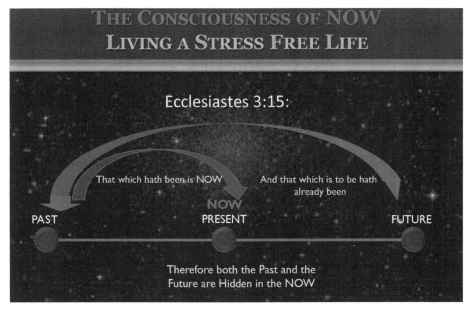

It suddenly dawned on me that the great King Solomon was not speaking in redundancy when he declares, *that which hath been (Past) is __now__; and that which is to be (Future) hath already been (Past).* Being the wisest man who has ever lived, he was giving us the master key to living a meaningful, stress-free life! The text also contains the mystery of how to master both the past and the future. *That which hath been (Past) is __now__;* has a two-fold meaning that we will now examine.

- *That which hath been (Past) is __now__;* means that all that is to be known about the PAST is hidden in God in the moment called Now! We can go to God at any given moment to unlock the PAST of a person or thing and He would gladly reveal it to us, if it serves His will. This is

75

exactly what the Lord Jesus Christ did with the Samaritan woman. He told her that she had five ex-husbands and the man she was currently living with was not her husband. In this case the woman's troubled "PAST" was hidden in Christ in the moment called Now!

- *That which hath been (Past) is <u>now;</u>* also means that the best place to resolve or heal the hurts, disappoints, fears and traumas of the PAST is the moment called Now! This is because the moment called "Now" is pregnant with the IAM presence of God. This is the main reason why Yeshua brought up the Samaritan woman's PAST. It was not to embarrass her with what He knew about her. He was summoning her PAST to help her bring it to Him in the "Now" so He could heal her from it. He wanted her to know that she was not defined by her PAST failures but by her inherent destiny in Christ in God!

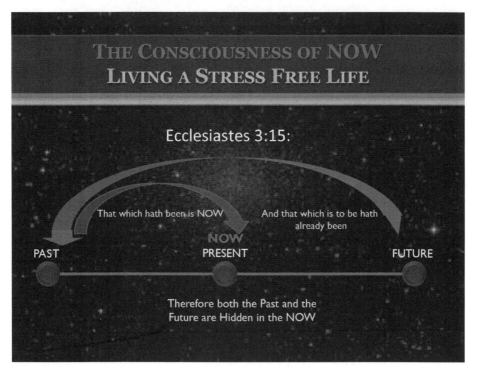

Let us know re-examine this powerful passage from the book of Ecclesiastes. *That which hath been (Past) is <u>now;</u> and that which is to be (Future) hath already been (Past).* Let us once again imagine a line with three time measurements, "Past, Present and Future" separated at equal distance. We will call these time measurements, "P1, P2 and F1." While we are stuck with the line, all of these time measurements have an equal measure of rule on people's consciousness. But imagine for a moment that suddenly the hand of

NAILS OF THE WORLD SPA
1445 S. ARIZONA AVE. #10
CHANDLER, AZ 85286
480-786-9700

03/04/2014   10:51:54
Merchant ID: XXXXXXXXXXXXX0232
Device ID: 1111
Terminal ID: PD04.

CREDIT CARD

VISA SALE

CARD #   XXXXXXXXXXXX4280
TRANS #   002
Batch #:   4
Approval Code: 162793
ACI Code: E
TRANS ID: 164063665621573
Entry Method: Swiped
Mode: Online

SALE AMOUNT $43.00

TIP AMOUNT   _____

TOTAL AMOUNT   _____

CUSTOMER COPY

God begins to draw a circular line through "P1" and "F1" and back through "P1." Suddenly our line is enclosed in a circle. Can you see what just happened? "P1 and F1" just disappeared into the circumference of the circle, because a circle is the only geometric figure that carries the characteristics of eternity-timelessness.

A circle has no beginning or ending. It has neither past nor future. At this point the only TIME measurement from the timeline we started with that still remains is "P2" which is the "Present or Now!" This means that the moment called "Now or Present" is the most defining essence of a circle. It's also the only point on the timeline that carries the characteristics of eternity. Both the past and future have a diminishing element to them while the moment called "Now or Present" is perpetually infinite. Now is always "Now" regardless of how many times you encounter it. This quickly explains why faith in God can only work in the "Now!" *Now, faith is the substance of things hoped for and the evidence of things not seen* (Hebrews 11:1). The Holy Spirit said to me, *"Son the moment you begin to live in the Now, you will begin to enjoy all the endless benefits of being part of the Circle of Life."* God consciousness is the essence of the Circle of Life. Everything God is and has is contained in the moment called "Now!"

Experiencing the Kingdom in the Now!

*Then shall the King say unto them on his right hand, Come, ye blessed of my Father, inherit the **kingdom** prepared for you from the foundation of the world:*

Matthew 25:34

In the above passage of scripture Yeshua makes it very clear that the blessing of the Heavenly Father is that we His dear children would inherit "His Kingdom." The Kingdom is our rightful and most prized inheritance. Something is only an inheritance if we did not work for it but a relative gave it to us. If we work for something its called wages but if it's given to us on the basis of a relationship its called inheritance. Our relationship with Jesus Christ has given us access to a most priceless inheritance- the Kingdom of God. Yeshua paid a heavy price on the cross to bequeath us this valuable inheritance. But there is a simple but deeply profound condition to enjoying this great inheritance. Many who have received this priceless inheritance short circuit this powerful blessing by failing to meet this simple obligation. We will now examine this simple condition for enjoying our inheritance.

"So don't worry about these things, saying, 'What will we eat? What will we drink? What will we wear?' 32 These things dominate the thoughts of unbelievers, but your heavenly Father already knows all your needs. 33 Seek the Kingdom of God above all else, and live righteously, and he will give you everything you need. Matthew 6:31-33

Jesus Christ introduces us to this unchanging condition for enjoying our inheritance by saying, *"So don't worry about these things, saying, 'what will we eat? What will we drink? What will we wear?' These things dominate the thoughts of unbelievers, but your heavenly Father already knows all your needs.* He introduces us to this condition by telling us not to do what we are most accustomed to doing- worrying. Many of us are masters at worrying about, *what we shall eat, what we will drink and what we will wear.* Yeshua is trying to introduce us to a "consciousness" that is beyond what we call "tangible reality." Much of what we call tangible reality is the biggest lie of all, because whatever is visible is temporal and whatever is invisible is everlasting.

Yeshua then introduces us to the predominant thoughts of Gentiles or unbelievers. *'What will we eat? What will we drink? What will we wear?' These things dominate the thoughts of unbelievers.* From the above statement its easy to see why millions in the world we live struggle to live in the "Now!" Thoughts about what we shall eat, what we shall drink and what we shall wear do not lend themselves to living in the "Now!" These thoughts are driven by the animal instinct to survive. These stress-causing thoughts are not driven by the engines of revelation. These thoughts lend themselves to a life of hustling for a living. But the antidote to this stress generating lifestyle is the unchanging condition for enjoying our blessed inheritance. Its found in the sentence...

Seek the Kingdom of God above all else, and live righteously, and he will give you everything you need. The unchanging condition of enjoying our blessed inheritance is "seeking first His Kingdom and His righteousness!" Why seek His Kingdom first? His Kingdom is a tangible reality found only in living in the moment called "Now!" The Kingdom is "Now," its power and provisions are all found in the IAM Presence of God that saturates the moment called "Now!" Righteousness means being in right standing with God. When God's children develop the consciousness of living in the "Now" they are aligning themselves with the government of God. In this place of compliance all of our needs we be met according to His riches in glory by Christ Jesus.

LIFE APPLICATION SECTION

MEMORY VERSE

Behold, I am with you and will keep you wherever you go, and will bring you back to this land; for I will not leave you until I have done what I have spoken to you." 16 Then Jacob awoke from his sleep and said, "Surely the Lord is in this place, and I did not know it."

Genesis 28:10-16 (NKJV)

1. What is worshipping the Future?

2. How can you break free of the Tyranny of the Past?

Chapter Nine

THE HEALING OF SOUL FRAGMENTATION

Soul fragmentation is the splitting, or advanced form of compartmentalization, of a person's soul. Soul fragmentation is the ultimate prize sought by demonic powers. There is no human being who can function properly, according to God's perfect design, when their Soul is fragmented. In the book of First Thessalonians, we are told that man is a triune being consisting of spirit, soul and body. Man's spirit gives him spiritual consciousness while his body gives him world consciousness. On the other hand, man's soul gives him self-consciousness making man's soul the seat of self-consciousness. Consequently, anything that fragments man's soul has a direct impact on his ability to realize and manifest his true self in Christ in God.

Now may the God of peace make you holy in every way, and may your whole spirit and soul and body be kept blameless until our Lord Jesus Christ comes again

(1 Thessalonians 5:23).

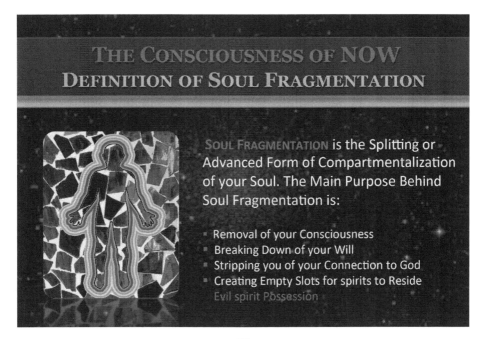

THE CONSCIOUSNESS OF NOW
DEFINITION OF SOUL FRAGMENTATION

SOUL FRAGMENTATION is the Splitting or Advanced Form of Compartmentalization of your Soul. The Main Purpose Behind Soul Fragmentation is:

- Removal of your Consciousness
- Breaking Down of your Will
- Stripping you of your Connection to God
- Creating Empty Slots for spirits to Reside
- Evil spirit Possession

LEVELS OF SOUL FRAGMENTATION

The main aim behind soul fragmentation is:

• *Removal of your consciousness*

• *Breaking of your will*

• *Stripping you of your connection to God*

• *Creating empty slots for spirits to reside*

• *Evil spirit possession*

"To understand soul fragmentation one also needs some comprehension related to remote linking, remote influence and spirit possession. Most consider this a sensitive topic, especially since it often leads to the discovery of soul ties. And the most difficult soul ties to break are the ones with family members. This could be why many are sensitive to the specific topic at hand, but my personal opinion is that most are simply not willing to take responsibility and have become like cloned sheep, living only for the purpose they have been programmed for. No longer can they remember their original state of consciousness but now, in their fallen capacity, they are simply part of the herd that follows the dictated road. Many are unable and not willing to wake up, having no desire to change, they, the sheep, are heading for the global takeover of the robot state where no real consciousness will exist and where you will only do what you are told and taught.

In this New World Order, there will be no link to a living God or any act of your divine creational birthright and free will, which is essential to truly living. You will be a robot if you follow this path controlled by stronger minds than yours, and what's worse, your presence in your body will no longer be required. Stop and wake up before it is too late. People were created with an individual capacity to connect to the Creator, live for and with Him. Do not discard your birthright for lower states of empty purposeless living, which only serve to open you up to death: death in the physical sense of disease and mental discomfort, and spiritual death in the form of spirit possession on so many levels. In the end if you follow the way of the sheep, there will be no "you," in your body, only them. Your vehicle (body) will belong to them. This takeover is a slow one and unless you start with some conscious decisions of claiming back your free will, it will quickly escalate into an almost unstoppable snowball effect."

WHAT IS SOUL FRAGMENTATION?

The Lord is my shepherd; I shall not want. ²He maketh me to lie down in green pastures: he leadeth me beside the still waters. ³He restoreth my soul: he leadeth me in the paths of righteousness for his name's sake (Psalm 23:1-3, KJV).

"The soul or the actual unique identity of the body is the driving force behind the vehicle (the body). The "soul" is what you consider to be "you." You think of yourself as the body, mind and all that encompasses it, and that is true; but the driving force is the soul. The body only becomes the major aspect if it is required for physical strength, or when in pain or discomfort; the mind becomes the major player when it needs to solve a complicated equation; and the heart or emotions, when any kind of feelings are involved. All these affect the soul on an individual and combined level. The soul is the predominant determining part and the soul is what becomes fragmented. If the soul is fragmented, all control over body, mind, and heart are influenced and distorted. In time, this external remote control can be on such an overpowering influential level that it will be termed "possession." The lower forms of control over your desires, lusts and other feelings, including your thoughts and ailments, are not termed possession by most. But it is one and the same. The operation is only at a lower level of detection and still influences and directs you in ways beyond your consciousness. These minor ways are enough for the thief (the devil) to steal from you!" (see- www.stopfollowingman.org)

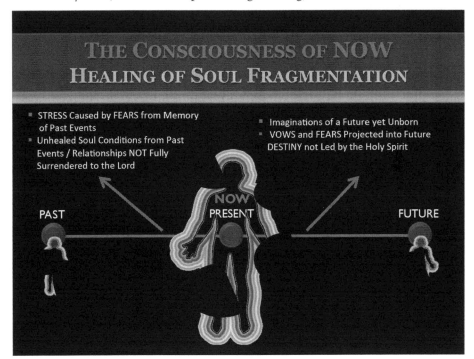

THE CONSCIOUSNESS OF NOW
HEALING OF SOUL FRAGMENTATION

- STRESS Caused by FEARS from Memory of Past Events
- Unhealed Soul Conditions from Past Events / Relationships NOT Fully Surrendered to the Lord

- Imaginations of a Future yet Unborn
- VOWS and FEARS Projected into Future DESTINY not Led by the Holy Spirit

PAST

NOW
PRESENT

FUTURE

I WILL NEVER MARRY A BLACK OR ASIAN MAN

"Now suppose a young woman makes a vow or binds herself with an impulsive pledge and later marries"

(Numbers 30:6).

My husband must have asked me to marry him at least seven times. Each time my answer was a deafening "NO," followed by a great excuse. *"I love your message. It is my desire to connect you with people I know in the ministry, as well as help you with your business ventures in the marketplace. But I don't believe I am your wife."* However as days went by, I felt the increasing but gentle nudging of the Holy Spirit towards Francis. There was a part of me that was opening up to the possibility that he was my husband, but my flesh was strongly resisting this possibility. As I continued to work for Francis, the Lord's voice started to get louder and I kept praying and asking Him to reveal the truth to me. One night while I was in prayer, the Lord reminded me of the visions I had about my husband in 2005. I was on a plane on my way to Mozambique, Africa when I had my first vision. First, I saw a big engagement ring suspended up in the air. All I could see was its surface. Then I saw a man prostrated on the surface of the ring. The Lord told me that this is my husband and it is the way he is positioned in the spirit. I had the rest of the visions a few days after we arrived in Mozambique. I saw Jesus and my husband sitting on the edge of the ring with their arms around each other's shoulder. Jesus and my husband were so happy talking and sharing and I could see their legs dangling back and forth. They clearly were having fun. Then I heard the Lord again, *"Your husband is my friend."* Then I saw a table with the communion elements. Jesus and my husband were having communion together. Suddenly I appeared and I shared communion with them.

As soon as the Lord reminded me about these visions, I knew that I could no longer deny the possibility of Francis being my husband. I had the vision in Africa and Francis is African. His relationship with the Lord is very evident even in his writing; he is a friend of God. And lastly, the Lord highlighted communion in my vision. Communion is a very important part of Francis' revelation on the Order of Melchizedek. Then I heard the Lord say, *"If you can't see your husband in the spirit, you cannot bring the things of the Spirit into manifestation!"* Let me tell you, the fear of God came upon me so that I cried out, *"Lord, so if Francis is my husband, then take me beyond time where You make everything beautiful. I have to see him the way You see him (see Ecclesiastes 3:11)."* The answer came one day while on our way back from a business meeting in Texas. Out of the blue, Francis felt we should pray for my niece, Katrina. As soon as I closed my eyes to pray for her, I was in the Spirit.

I saw the soul of my niece in the present, or the "Now," but it was fragmented. There were parts of her soul missing! Then I started to see the missing parts: some were in the past and some were in the future. I saw these parts behind a jail cell. It was as if Katrina was a prisoner of the past and of the future. Then a very thick presence of God came upon us. We started to travail and shake in the Spirit. Immediately the Spirit led me to call back my niece's fragmented soul pieces from the future and the past back into the "Now." I prayed, "Lord, we call Katrina's soul pieces that are stuck in the past back into the Now. Lord, we call her soul that is stuck in the future back into the Now!" Then I heard Him say, *"Don't just call her soul back. Be specific and also call her mind, will and emotions back into the Now."* So we prayed, *"Lord, we call Katrina's soul pieces that are stuck in the past and in the future into the now! We call her mind, will and emotions back into the Now!"* Once we finished praying for my niece, the Lord instructed us to call back our own fragmented soul pieces from the past and present back into the now. Then He instructed us to repent for allowing our souls to be fragmented. We repented and asked for His forgiveness.

I must say that this is one of the most powerful encounters I've ever had with the Lord. I went to bed in total peace. However, when I woke up, I was surprised! I knew, and I knew without a shadow of the doubt, that Francis was to be my husband! I heard in the spirit, *"Can a nation be birthed in one day? Yes, I can change your heart in one day."* It was very clear to me that the shift in my mindset and my heart happened when we called fragments of our soul back into the Now. The Lord explained to me that part of my issue was the vow I had made, *"I will never marry an Asian or a Black man."* A vow of "I will" indicates some time in the future. I don't have any racial issues with these ethnicities, as I am an Asian myself. It was just a personal preference as there was a particular look I was always attracted to. I must say, it was the biggest deception I have ever accepted in my life. As soon as our soul is fragmented, there is a removal of consciousness and a breakdown of the will. In my case, my consciousness to be open to marrying a black man had been affected by my vow. It was replaced by a particular look based on my own fleshly desire. Because of this, my will resisted strongly to the notion that marrying a black man could be God's plan for my life. Therefore, no matter what Francis did I could not see him as my future mate!

EMOTIONAL TRIGGERING MECHANISMS

"Soul fragmentation is the opening(s) where the minor program slots reside. *A program is anything that can be triggered to make you function in a specific way.* This could be an emotional reaction, a thought train or a bodily function or reaction. More complicated programs work in alternating or reoccurring sequences combining all the aforementioned." (see- www.stopfollowingman.org)

And it came to pass on the morrow, that the evil spirit from God came upon Saul, and he prophesied in the midst of the house: and David played with his hand, as at other times: and there was a javelin in Saul's hand. [11]And Saul cast the javelin; for he said, I will smite David even to the wall with it. And David avoided out of his presence twice

(1 Samuel 18:10-11, KJV).

Soul fragmentation is the separation or the creation of a separate compartment in your soul from where influence can be exerted. People fail to see that emotions are generated and can be influenced and controlled in all ways. Most fragmentation occurs from an emotionally manipulated aspect or rather some overpowering experience. Emotions are the most important aspect by which we, as people, function.

We live in a very emotional world. All you have to do is turn on the television and you will hear news about crimes of passion that are committed on a daily basis all over the world. Even our political climate is desperately toxic as politicians from each side of the political divide blame the other party for all that ails our emotionally divided country. You don't have to be a rocket scientist to figure out why emotional triggering mechanisms are one of the devil's favorite weapons in the "War on Consciousness." In highly emotional situations, our IQ (intelligence quotient) goes way down while our EQ (emotional quotient) rises radically. In such moments, most people lose sight of consciousness. Under the overpowering influence of toxic emotional stimuli, we become susceptible to demonically engineered remote control having given up consciousness in the heat of the moment.

Jailhouses are filled with men and women who are serving time because of something they did in the heat of the moment. Under the influence of high emotional stress and upheaval, they shot and killed somebody they loved or the person with whom they had an altercation. In the aftermath of the emotional upheaval, after they regained their consciousness, they are shocked to discover what they did during the emotional upheaval. What is worse, the matter that triggered their emotional outburst was not all that important and, in most cases, the actual offense was dismal in the light of their violent emotional outburst. How many people do you know who would allow themselves to be manipulated by their emotions if they knew that the price of such an emotional upheaval would be the loss of consciousness?

In the above passage of Scripture, we are given a front row seat in the story of King Saul who hired David to be his official minstrel in the royal courts after the young man killed the Philistine giant Goliath. The Bible tells us that every time David was playing the harp, the tormenting spirit from the Lord that was oppressing the King would leave him immediately. One day, when David and King Saul were coming from battle they were welcomed at the gates to the City by a troop of women who were dancing and singing songs about the returning warriors. The women declared that King Saul had killed his thousands but David had killed his tens of thousands. When King Saul heard that the women of Israel were ascribing more victories to David than they were ascribing to him, he immediately became deeply offended. From that moment on, he eyed David enviously. I believe that from that point, King Saul's soul went into a place of fragmentation because he could not get past that particular event. Parts of his soul pieces became stuck in that time frame and a demonic looping of that event played constantly in his mind until his hatred for David became uncontrollable. The Bible tells us that one day while David was playing his harp to sooth the ailing King, the King suddenly stood up and threw a javelin at David and almost killed him. This happened twice; each time the jealous King repented and he declared that he would never do it again. But it was clear that King Saul had no control over how he felt towards David emotionally. He was already emotionally compromised through the fear that David would take his kingdom from him because of the songs he was told the women were singing.

SOUL TIES

And it came to pass, when he had made an end of speaking unto Saul, that the soul of Jonathan was knit with the soul of David, and Jonathan loved him as his own soul

(1 Samuel 18:1, KJV).

"A soul tie is like a linkage in the soul realm between two people. It links their souls together, which can bring forth either beneficial results or negative results.

The positive effect of a soul tie: In a godly marriage, God links the two together and the Bible tells us that they become one flesh. As a result of the two becoming one flesh, they are bound together and will cleave to one another in a unique way. The purpose of this cleaving is to build a very healthy, strong and close relationship between a man and a woman.

"And said, For this cause shall a man leave father and mother, and shall cleave to his wife: and they twain shall be one flesh"

(Matthew 19:5, KJV). [Emphasis added]

Soul ties can also be found in strong or close friendships. They are not just limited to marriage, as we can see with King David and Jonathan:

"And it came to pass, when he had made an end of speaking unto Saul, that <u>the soul of Jonathan was knit with the soul of David</u>, and Jonathan loved him as his own soul" (1 Samuel 18:1, KJV). [Emphasis added]

The negative effect of a soul tie: Soul ties can also be used for the devil's advantage. Soul ties formed from sex outside of marriage cause a person to become defiled.

> *"And when Shechem the son of Hamor the Hivite, prince of the country, saw her, he took her, and <u>lay with her, and defiled her. And his soul cleaved unto Dinah</u> the daughter of Jacob, and he loved the damsel, and spoke kindly unto the damsel"*
>
> *(Genesis 34:2-3, KJV). [Emphasis added]*

This is why it is so common for a person to still have "feelings" towards an ex-lover that they have no right to be attracted to in that way. Even twenty years down the road, a person may still think of their first lover - even if he or she is across the country and has their own family, all because of a soul tie! The following is an example of the result of an ungodly soul tie.

Demonic spirits can also take advantage of ungodly soul ties, and use them to transfer spirits between one person to another. I remember one young man I led through deliverance; he was facing severe demonic visitations and torment, all thanks to an ungodly soul tie. I led him to break the soul tie, and the attacks stopped completely!" *(Article from www.ministeringdeliverance.com)*

> *"And the Babylonians came to her into the bed of love, and <u>they defiled her with their whoredom, and she was polluted with them</u>"*
>
> *(Ezekiel 23:17, KJV). [Emphasis added]*

It is clear that negative soul ties can easily lead to "Soul fragmentation" as one person's soul pieces remain attached to another person's soul after the demise of the relationship. This is especially true in romantic relationships that go sour after a breakdown of a relationship. In 2012, the world was stunned by the famous murder case of Jodi Arias, a beautiful young woman from Arizona who plotted and carried out the vicious slaughter of her past boyfriend. If she was not going to have him, neither would any other woman. During the trial, she told a frustrated prosecutor that she could hardly remember the details of the carnage of that terrible day. Many thought she was faking her memory loss but I understood that she was robbed of consciousness because of the unhealthy soul tie with her past boyfriend; she was an easy prey for remote control by demonic entities. It is very plausible that during the carnage, she gave up consciousness due to her deeply fragmented soul condition and her body became simply a vehicle of those other spirits.

THE SPIRIT OF JEZEBEL AND SOUL TIES

Jezebel uses the bewitching powers of seduction to lure her victims and create **soul ties**. The Jezebel spirit is a strong man spirit. What is in you that the Jezebel spirit can see? She works a network of demon powers to climb her ladder of control. Some of the arrows in her quiver that create **soul ties** include the spirit of witchcraft, the spirit of divination, and the spirit of seduction. Jezebel is a master of seduction. The word "seduction" means literally to lead astray. It is a deliberate step-by-step process of temptation and enticement causing someone to do something they would not normally do. The spirit of seduction and the spirit of witchcraft are cousins. They are a similar class of evil spirits both used by the spirit of Jezebel.

THE BAIT OF JEZEBEL THAT CREATES SOUL TIES

The following article, written by Apostle Jonas Clark, clearly explains the process of the Jezebel spirit creating soul ties in a person.

"How does this spirit create soul ties? When Jezebel releases the spirit of seduction, **a "spiritual force" is released against your mind, imagination, and emotions.** Just as a fisherman may use various baits and lures so does the Jezebel spirit. Her baits and lures are all seductive in nature. Seduction is the bait that leads to a soul tie. You are the fish.

The purpose of the seduction is to create soul ties that can be used to control you. A soul tie is a spiritual or emotional attachment to another person. In this case, the bond is with a demonic spirit called Jezebel. Soul ties can be created in a myriad of ways such as:

- Sexual relationships

- Emotional manipulation

- Shared life experiences

- Personal tragedies

- Loss of a loved one

- Flattery of the prideful

- Consoling another

- Reaching out to the lonely

- Agreeing with Jezebel's offenses, hurts, wounds, and unforgiveness towards those in authority or leadership.

- Financial crisis.

Once soul ties have been established, Jezebel's victim becomes a eunuch. A eunuch is a child of the Jezebel spirit. This has nothing to do with the male gender. A castrated male, for example, is a eunuch. In other words, a eunuch is a person without strength that can no longer reproduce. A Jezebel eunuch has no life outside the controlling world of Jezebel. Again, a eunuch has no strength of their own, looks to the Jezebel spirit for approval, instruction, validation, and companionship." *(Article by Apostle Jonas Clark)*

HEALING FROM SOUL FRAGMENTATION IN THE NOW!

That which hath been is now; and that which is to be hath already been; and God requireth that which is past

(Ecclesiastes 3: 15, KJV).

Praise God that there is healing for soul fragmentation in the moment called "Now"! We have already made it clear in a previous chapter that the only point on the timeline, which is synonymous with "eternity" is the moment on the timeline called "Now or Present." The word "Present" is a derivative of the word "Presence." Consequently, the moment called "Now" has the highest concentration of the "Presence of God." This is because God is a God who created time but does not live in it. God has no immediate past or future because He is not governed by TIME. God exists in the zone of timelessness. So if we want to meet with God's glory, presence and power we must seek such an experience in the moment called "Now."

*God is our refuge and strength, a very **present** help in trouble*

(Psalm 46:1, KJV).

Much of the "Soul Fragmentation" that people go through happens within the "Timeline" of Time continuum. This is how the process of soul fragmentation normally happens: **Person-A** goes through a relationship breakdown or any other trauma, and a piece of his or her soul remains stuck to that past painful event. If these types of incidences repeat themselves a couple of times, soul fragmentation happens to **Person-A**. Person-A, who has now gone through these vicious life cycles suddenly has several past life events that collectively hold a piece of his or her soul. The diagram below will help illustrate this important point.

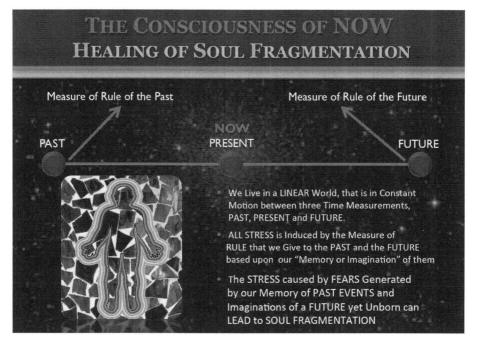

Let us now suppose that **Person-A** behaves like most humans. **Person-A,** reacting to past painful events decides to make a vow in order to protect themselves from being hurt again. The only problem with such a vow is that no human being is capable of protecting oneself without imprisoning himself or herself in the same shell they choose to hide in to avoid being hurt by others. The LORD is the only One who can truly protect us from others and ourselves. Since "Vows" always involve the future, in order to sustain a vow the person making the vow must make a conscious choice to sell pieces of their soul to securing the future event to which they are projecting their soul.

> *Some time later, the Lord spoke to Abram in a vision and said to him, "Do not be afraid, Abram, for I will protect you, and your reward will be great"*

(Genesis 15:1).

The cumulative effect of having soul pieces of **Person-A** stuck to the "Past or Future" creates a condition of serious "Soul Fragmentation," resulting in the removal of "consciousness" in the life of **Person-A.** A person such as this, no matter how sincere, cannot achieve "full consciousness," because too much of their soul is not present in the "Now" where they can fully engage the presence of God. But if such a person can begin to call all of their soul pieces that are stuck to the past or future into the "Now" through the Blood of Christ, their healing will begin immediately. There is soul restoration in the "Now" because it is the only point in the timeline where mankind can truly engage the presence, power and glory of the Living of God. It is time for you to live in the "Now" and enjoy maximum exposure to the presence of God.

LIFE APPLICATION SECTION

MEMORY VERSE

"And when Shechem the son of Hamor the Hivite, prince of the country, saw her, he took her, and <u>lay with her, and defiled her. And his soul cleaved unto Dinah</u> the daughter of Jacob, and he loved the damsel, and spoke kindly unto the damsel"

(Genesis 34:2-3, KJV). [Emphasis added]

1. What is Soul Fragmentation?

2. How can "Living in the Now" help bring about the healing of "Soul fragmentation?"

Chapter Ten

CALLING THOSE THINGS THAT BE NOT

(As it is written, I have made thee a father of many nations,) before him whom he believed, even God, who quickeneth the dead, and calleth those things, which be not as though they were. 18Who against hope believed in hope, that he might become the father of many nations, according to that which was spoken, So shall thy seed be. 19And being not weak in faith, he considered not his own body now dead, when he was about an hundred years old, neither yet the deadness of Sarah's womb: 20 He staggered not at the promise of God through unbelief; but was strong in faith, giving glory to God

(Romans 4:17-20, KJV).

One of the primary benefits of "Living in the Now" is how this spiritual positioning quickly engages our faith. This kind of living ignites the God-kind-of-faith. From the above Scripture passage, we will examine how living in the "Now" brings us into a place of fulfilled destiny. This passage is rich with things that happen when living in that place of unbroken communion with God in the place called "Now." We will now dissect this powerful passage of Scripture.

(As it is written, I have made thee a father of many nations,) before him whom he believed, even God, who quickeneth the dead, and calleth those things, which be not as though they were. 18 Who against hope believed in hope, that he might become the father of many nations, according to that which was spoken, So shall thy seed be. 19 And being not weak in faith, he considered not his own body now dead, when he was about an hundred years old, neither yet the deadness of Sarah's womb: 20 He staggered not at the promise of God through unbelief; but was strong in faith, giving glory to God;

IT IS WRITTEN

The expression *"As it is written"* in the above text, brings us face-to-face with one of the primary benefits of "Living in the Now." *"As it is written,"* means that when we begin to live in the "Now" we will begin to walk in everything that was written about us in the records of heaven from before the foundation of the world! We stop living a life of trial and error and we enter a season of total accuracy in how we must fulfill our Kingdom assignment here on earth. Like Jesus, we will say, "...I come (in the volume of the book it is written of me,) to do thy will, O God,!" (Hebrews 10:7, KJV). There is perhaps nothing more tragic than being number one at a race we were not called to run. Yeshua was very sure about who He was and what He was born to do. Why is the Body of Christ full of believers who are so confused about the depth, height and width of their inherent destiny? When we learn to live in the "Now" we quickly begin to discover what is written about us.

FATHER OF MANY NATIONS

The expression *"I have made thee a father of many nations"* literally means that God can only form and fashion us into an instrument He can use to advance His Kingdom when we "Live in the Now." But the statement also shows us the method He uses to transform us in accordance with His predetermined purpose for our life. God uses a past present tense to describe Abraham's spiritual position, *"I have made thee..."* even though in the natural Abraham was not yet the father of many nations. In the natural Isaac was yet to be born.

By addressing Abraham, not as he was in the natural but as he was in Christ in God, God reconditioned Abraham's spirit, soul and body to enter into God's predetermined will for his life. The reason God deals with Abraham as though he had already become what God had set him out to be in His foreknowledge is because there is no past or future in the moment called "Now." This being the case, God was treating Abraham as He saw him - complete and perfect in Christ!

> *And there came an angel of the Lord, and sat under an oak which was in Ophrah, that pertained unto Joash the Abiezrite: and his son Gideon threshed wheat by the winepress, to hide it from the Midianites. 12And the angel of the Lord appeared unto him, and said unto him, The Lord is with thee, thou mighty man of valour*
>
> *(Judges 6:11-12, KJV).*

We see God using this same principle to transform Gideon's life. When the angel of the Lord appeared to Gideon, he is hiding in the winepress treading wheat, terrified of the Midianites. In the natural, he was just as scared as the rest of Israel. But instead of addressing him as a coward, the angel of the Lord calls him a "Mighty Man of Valor." In the natural, the angel's statement seemed to be out of touch with reality. What the angel told Gideon was either a falsehood or a revelation. But the truth of the matter is that the angel of God was simply calling Gideon into the fellowship of the "Now." He was calling Gideon as God saw him in the "Now" in Christ in God. Based upon this heavenly perspective, Gideon was truly a man of valor. Living in the "Now" will awaken us to what we are in Christ in God and not as we see ourselves.

FAITH THAT ARRESTS GOD

The expression *"before him whom he believed, even God,"* introduces us to another fascinating aspect of "Living in the Now." Living in the "Now" is a faith-fueled life that is lived out in the presence of God. This expression intimates a faith-filled life that is driven by the engines of intimacy with God. This does not suggest faith in the abstract. It suggests the ability to stand before God in living faith and living color. It also suggests, or denotes, the kind of faith that is rooted in God as its primary objective. This kind of faith is very different from the "faith" we see in much of Christendom, which is a "faith" that is rooted in "things or in spiritual giftedness" but not in God. Living in the "Now" inspires in us the kind of faith that arrests God himself.

> And he said, Let me go, for the day breaketh. And he said, I will not let thee go, except thou bless me. ²⁷And he said unto him, What is thy name? And he said, Jacob. ²⁸And he said, Thy name shall be called no more Jacob, but Israel: for as a prince hast thou power with God and with men, and hast prevailed
>
> (Genesis 32:26-28, KJV).

Jacob experienced the kind of faith that we are talking about when the Angel of the Lord appeared to him on the river Jabbok. The Bible declares that Jacob wrestled with this divine being the whole night. Jacob passionately declared, "I will not let you go until you bless me." Jacob's faith had found God and he was determined not to let go until he experienced a life-altering change. He fought by faith with the Angel of the Lord until the "breaking of a new day." Finally, the angel of the Lord asked what his name was. Why would the Angel ask for his name? I believe it was to show us that no man's nature remains the same when any person enters the moment called "Now," where their spirit engages God in a very real way.

THE QUICKENING ANOINTING

The expression *"even God, who quickeneth the dead,"* is another very interesting aspect of "Living in the Now." The expression *"even God, who quickeneth the dead,"* means that the moment called "Now" is saturated with the spirit of resurrection! This makes sense because the moment called "Now" is saturated with the "I AM" Presence of God. This means that when we are conscious that we are living in the "Now," we will begin to draw upon the spirit of resurrection. Things, gifts, dreams, visions and talents that were dead will begin to come alive. Nothing dies in the presence of God. This is why Jesus told Mary and Martha, "I am the life and the resurrection!" Living in the "Now" will begin to reverse the technology of death in our lives and over our businesses. The word "quicken" means, "to give life to!" God wants to give life to everything you touch if you would dare live in the "Now." Even Aaron's dead stick came to life once it slept inside the Ark of the Covenant.

SOVEREIGN ATTRACTION

Finally the expression, *"and calleth those things, which be not as though they were"* adds another very exciting layer to the power of "Living in the Now." This expression introduces us to one of the most powerful phenomenon for attracting the blessings of God: a divine phenomenon known as "Sovereign Attraction." My dear friend, Dr. Gordon Bradshaw, has written extensively on this phenomenon in his best selling book: *Authority for Assignment*. In his book, he makes it clear that "Sovereign Attraction" is far better than "Karma." God orchestrates the former, while the latter is orchestrated by nature.

Sovereign attraction is a supernatural force field of divine favor, blessings, promotion and power. It is a supernatural force field that is the by-product of being in a place that is saturated with the "I AM" Presence of God. Since God is the God of the "Now," His presence is most felt in the "Now." Consequently, when we begin to live in the "Now," it is like stepping into the eye of the storm. The strongest part of the storm bombards us; except in this scenario, the "storm is the Presence of God." Since everything in creation is attracted to the Presence of God, "Sovereign Attraction" happens to people who have mastered the "Consciousness of Now!"

LIFE APPLICATION SECTION
MEMORY VERSE

(As it is written, I have made thee a father of many nations,) before him whom he believed, even God, who quickeneth the dead, and calleth those things, which be not as though they were. [18] Who against hope believed in hope, that he might become the father of many nations, according to that which was spoken, So shall thy seed be. [19] And being not weak in faith, he considered not his own body now dead, when he was about an hundred years old, neither yet the deadness of Sarah's womb: [20] He staggered not at the promise of God through unbelief; but was strong in faith, giving glory to God

(Romans 4:17-20, KJV).

1. What is Sovereign Attraction?

2. How does God treat us when we step into the Now?

Chapter Eleven

THE WITCHCRAFT OF NEEDS

"Lord, what's happening with the desolation that I am seeing in the Body of Christ?" I had asked the Lord several times. I had seen anointed men and women of God make choices that sabotaged their very powerful God given destinies. I was quite disturbed by the trend that I was seeing and wanted answers directly from the throne of God. The answer came months later while I was visiting Bishop Robert E. Smith in Little Rock, Arkansas.

There was nothing extraordinary about that night when I went to sleep in the prophet's chamber prepared by Bishop Robert E. Smith. But what happened in the wee hours of the morning changed my life and collective "consciousness" completely. I woke up suddenly to a spiritual experience I will never forget. When I woke up it was though I was in the center of the eye of the storm. Everything around me was spinning out of control.

Since this was not a natural tornado I knew that the swirling I was feeling all around me was spiritual in nature. I was suddenly overcome by an overwhelming sense of neediness. I became acutely aware that I had so many unmet needs. I was so overcome by the magnitude of my unmet needs that I panicked. My panic soon turned into a ferocious contemplation of suicide. Anybody who knows me knows that I am usually a very positive minded individual with little time for defeatist sentimentalities. But for the first time in my life I seriously contemplated suicide.

Furthermore while I was going through this spiritual tornado all awareness of the presence of God completely escaped me. I was acting like a person without Christ and without God. Suddenly everything was calm. The storm and the swirling of the room I was sleeping in stopped suddenly. I quickly recovered my usual upbeat disposition. "Lord what was that?" I asked apprehensively. The answer came quickly and it radically transformed me. *"What you just experienced is a demonic technology called, 'The Witchcraft of needs.' It's a demonic technology that causes people of destiny to abandon their destiny because of their felt needs. This technology is the source of much of the desolation that you are seeing in the Body of Christ."* I was stunned and remained speechless, pondering what I had just heard.

THE OCTOPUS

"Son, this demonic technology looks like an Octopus and it's also in you!" The Holy Spirit declared. I was completely stunned. Suddenly the hand of the Lord reached into my chest cavity and pulled out what looked like an "Octopus." I felt like a deeply rooted tree had just been plucked out of me. The effect of this divine surgery was very real. The Holy Spirit showed me that the "Witchcraft of needs" robs people of "God consciousness" and replaces it with "need consciousness." God becomes smaller in their minds while the size of their needs grew exponentially. This explains why so many self-proclaimed followers of Christ struggle to stay in peace. Their minds are completely captivated by their felt needs. So much so that many followers of Christ cannot function in the "Now!" They are too busy worrying about the future to truly enjoy God's presence in the "Now!"

YOU CANNOT SERVE TWO MASTERS

> *No man can serve two masters: for either he will hate the one, and love the other; or else he will hold to the one, and despise the other. Ye cannot serve God and mammon.*

> Matthew 6:24 (KJV)

Jesus Christ in the above text introduces us to a very powerful principle that we must truly understand. *No man can serve two masters: for either he will hate the one, and love the other;* Jesus declared. This means that a person can never obsess about their past without forfeiting their focused engagement of the moment called "Now!" If a person is constantly worrying about tomorrow (the future) they can't possibly master the present. They are too divided between the future and the "Now!" Ultimately their obsession with their felt needs triumphs and the moment called "Now" in their life is greatly diminished. This is why the "Consciousness of Now" is about personal mastery of the "Now" by refusing to be taken out of our place of peace into the chaos of worrying about tomorrow!

TAKE NO THOUGHT FOR YOUR LIFE

> *Therefore I say unto you, Take no thought for your life, what ye shall eat, or what ye shall drink; nor yet for your body, what ye shall put on. Is not the life more than meat, and the body than raiment? 26 Behold the fowls of the air: for they sow not, neither do they reap, nor gather*

into barns; yet your heavenly Father feedeth them. Are ye not much better than they? 27 Which of you by taking thought can add one cubit unto his stature?

Matthew 6:25-27 KJV

In the above passage of Scripture Yeshua makes a staggering statement. He admonishes all His faithful disciples not to *"take thought about their life."* This is another way of saying, *"do not worry about your life."* For millions of people on our troubled planet this is an impossible task. Mankind is prone to worrying and fretting. *"Surely we are only human if we worry about tomorrow?"* But this is a lie from the bottomless pit. This is because we live in a world of "cause and effect." Worrying will not give birth to peace but to more worrying.

But if the "Witchcraft of needs" is a reality in our life it will be difficult for us to stay in a place of rest. The Octopus machinery behind our felt needs will continue to sway our attention back and forth. We need to ask the Holy Spirit to give us a divine surgery from this demonic technology. By telling us not to *"Take thought about our life;"* Jesus was making it clear that the fuel for this demonic technology is our "unsanctified thoughts about our future." We are to take every thought captive to the obedience of Christ; before they become strongholds in our mind.

THE CURSE OF LITTLE FAITH

Wherefore, if God so clothe the grass of the field, which to day is, and to morrow is cast into the oven, shall he not much more clothe you, O ye of little faith?

Matthew 6:30

Yeshua delves into a very compelling argument and makes a comparison between mankind and the grass of the field. He states emphatically that if the heavenly Father clothes the grass of field that has a very short life span; how can He fail to clothe His most prized possession? Man is God's crown jewel. The great King David declares in the Psalms, *"What is man that you are so mindful of him?"* King David was baffled by how much attention God lavishes on man.

But the million-dollar question is why don't most Christians believe this? Jesus gives us the answer in the above passage, "they suffer from the curse of little faith!" After many years of walking with the Lord I have come to the sobering conclusion that it is better to have "no faith" than to have "little faith."

The reason for this is obvious, but I will explain. When a person knows that they have no faith they can be persuaded into a place of functional faith. But when a person has "little faith" they know just enough to delude themselves into thinking that they are actually walking and living by faith. Such people are easily swayed between two opinions. People such as this can never stop the "Witchcraft of needs" from having a field day with them. I pray that the faith to move mountains and live in the "Now" will be birthed in your spirit while you are reading this book.

DON'T THINK LIKE A GENTILE

Therefore take no thought, saying, What shall we eat? or, What shall we drink? or, Wherewithal shall we be clothed? 32 (For after all these things do the Gentiles seek:) for your heavenly Father knoweth that ye have need of all these things.

Matthew 6:31-32

The Lord Jesus Christ goes further in an effort to help shift our "consciousness" towards our "felt needs." Jesus diagnoses the reason why so many people are so obsessed with worrying about the future. They think like Gentiles or heathens. When we worry constantly about our well being we are operating at the same level of consciousness as the people of this fallen world.

The world we live in is all about survival, instead of inspired destiny. The most common instinct is survival at any cost. The problem with this demonic mentality is that it assumes that God has not fully secured the "future" so it's up to us to hustle our way into an uncertain future. What a lie from the very pit of hell! God secured our future from before the foundation of the world. He also secured it again when Christ bled to death on the cross. To continue on our current path of stress and striving is to perpetuate the same demonic lack mentality that afflicts heathens.

THE ANTIDOTE

But seek ye first the kingdom of God, and his righteousness; and all these things shall be added unto you.

Matthew 6:33 KJV

I am so glad that we serve a God who does not correct us without giving us an antidote to our dilemma. After making very compelling arguments against what I call "stress consciousness," Jesus offers a solid solution. He admonishes us to change our primary pursuits from our felt-needs to "seeking His Kingdom and His righteousness." He admonishes to make this pursuit the first and most important pursuit of our entire existence here on earth.

What makes this stress-killing antidote Jesus is proposing so potent is that it has the power to radically alter our personal economy. Jesus says that if we seek His Kingdom and His righteousness *"everything else that we need to live a life of manifest destiny will be added to us!"* Yeshua says that all of these "things" will be added to you. What "things" is He referencing here? The "things" that He is referring to includes the following, *"what we shall wear, what we shall eat and what we shall drink"* to say the least. The "things" obviously include every aspect of provision necessary for any child of God to live an abundant life.

Finally the antidote to our stress driven culture is rooted in the fact that the Kingdom of God is only made readily available when we live in the moment called "Now!" The Kingdom and His righteousness is "Now." This divine experience cannot be postponed or relegated to the past. The Kingdom of God is as potent today as it was two thousand years ago when the Messiah roamed the earth. Its is truly the "Kingdom of the Now!" Don't allow the witchcraft of needs to rob of you of the joy of living in His presence daily!

LIMITLESS PROVISION FROM A ROOT OUT OF DRY GROUND

Who hath believed our report? and to whom is the arm of the Lord revealed?2 For he shall grow up before him as a tender plant, and as a root out of a dry ground:

Isaiah 53:1-2 (KJV)

In my humble opinion there is no scripture in the entire Old Testament that is as powerful as the above passage of scripture in easing our fears is about the subject of Divine provision. The prophet Isaiah begins by asking a very important question, *"Who has believed our report? To whom has the arm of the Lord been revealed?"* The prophet's questions carry the implicit warning that if we do not take it to heart to believe the report of the Lord concerning what He has declared in His Word about His ability to provide for us we are not going to break the witchcraft of needs of over our consciousness. We will be harassed constantly by our felt needs and fail to live in the consciousness of the moment called "Now."

But what is most startling about this passage of Scripture is the second part of the verse that declares *"he shall grow up before him as a tender plant, and as a root out of a dry ground."* This expression is very powerful indeed because it carries the mystery of how to live a life of supernatural abundance in Christ Jesus. It is common knowledge that if a tender plant and root are planted into the ground their nutrients and water supply come from the ground. But what the prophet of God is proposing here is completely out of the box and revolutionary. He describes Jesus as a tender plant and root that grows out of dry ground. How can a tender plant and a root thrive in dry ground? The prophetic meaning behind his expression is simply this, the prophet Isaiah sees Jesus Christ as a the root out of dry ground that is not gathering its resources from the ground. To the contrary the tender plant and root are the ones giving life to the lifeless ground. Suddenly it made sense to me. If Christ is a tender plant and root out of dry ground; there is no way that He will be looking for provision from his own creation. Since the ground is part of God's creation when you plant Christ into the soil of any ground Christ will begin to give life to your economy. This is why when Christ is planted in any soul or dry ground you will experience much fruit in every area of your life.

LIFE APPLICATION SECTION

Memory Verse

*Behold, I am with you and will keep you wherever you go, and will bring you back to this land; for I will not leave you until I have done what I have spoken to you." **16** Then Jacob awoke from his sleep and said, "Surely the Lord is in this place, and I did not know it."*

Genesis 28:10-16 (NKJV)

1. What is the Witchcraft of Needs?

2. What antidote did Jesus suggest to heal our worries?

Chapter Twelve

BREAKING THE TIME BARRIER

From antiquity to the present times men and women have constantly grappled with the ever-lingering issue of their own mortality. The sudden death of a co-worker, friend or a family member only serves to amplify the feeling of man's inevitable appointment with his greatest nemesis- death. Men of all races, creed or political affiliation hate death. Death is a constant and painful reminder that we are living on borrowed "TIME." Once again its "TIME" that seems to be pulling the strings of our fragile existence. How many men and women have looked death in the eye while wishing they just had more "TIME" to finish some unfinished business.

"The time will come," says the Lord, "when the grain and grapes will grow faster than they can be harvested. Then the terraced vineyards on the hills of Israel will drip with sweet wine!

Amos 9:13

While its true that in this fallen world, "TIME" has mastery over the affairs of men; this statement does not have to be true for citizens of the Kingdom of God. As we have already stated mankind was never created to serve "TIME." To the contrary "TIME" was created to serve God and man. But ever since the fall of Adam and Eve "TIME" exercises great mastery over mankind even to the extent of deciding the TIME of his mortality. But I have good news for you! The prophet Amos in the ninth chapter declares, *"The TIME will come," says the Lord, "when the grain and grapes will grow faster than they can be harvested."* This is a very powerful and revolutionary prophetic statement. The only way grain and grapes can grow faster than they can be harvested is when the "TIME Barrier" between the "Seed" and "Harvest" collapses!

THE CONSCIOUSNESS OF NOW
BREAKING THE TIME BARRIER

- *ECCLESIASTES 3:1-10* shows us that TIME itself is in a FALLEN STATE.

- TIME is in a Fallen State because the Instrument of TIME has become an Open Portal for both Divine and Demonic Technologies.

- TIME is King and Lord over whatever Falls under or Enters its Sphere of Authority.

- The Malfunction of TIME has Opened a Doorway for an Avalanche of Demonic Technologies that Create STRUGGLE and STRESS in People's Lives.

SEEDTIME AND HARVEST

While the earth remaineth, seedtime and harvest, and cold and heat, and summer and winter, and day and night shall not cease. Genesis 8:22 KJV

After the flood that came in Noah's day and destroyed that ancient world of sin, God made a very powerful decree that would forever change man's relationship to "TIME." Instead of "TIME" serving man as it did before the fall, man was to serve "TIME" in order to exact a harvest from the earth. "TIME" would forever stand between man's seed and his harvest as an executor of his God given inheritance. But the decree from the mouth of God also contains one of the most powerful keys for breaking the "TIME Barrier" that for the most part delays the manifestation of many of the promises that God wants His people to enjoy. This powerful spiritual key for reversing much of the mastery that "TIME" has on man's harvest or posterity is contained in the expression, "*While the earth remaineth.*"

"*While the earth remaineth*" means that "TIME" only has mastery over the process of seeding and harvesting while "Natural law" remains the predominant technology behind how a person creates his or her income. While *natural law remains* the "seed" that is planted in the soil of the earth must go through the natural process of maturation. But this statement also means that when we transcend through the Spirit of God the power of "Natural law" we can break any "TIME barrier" between our seed and harvest. I believe that this scenario is what the prophet Amos was foreseeing when he was declaring that the "TIME" is coming when the grapes will grow faster than they can be harvested. The TIME barrier is about to collapse so the Body of Christ can enter into a season of unprecedented supernatural abundance like the world has never seen before.

REDISCOVERING GOD'S ORIGINAL INTENT

And God said, Let us make man in our image, after our likeness: and let them have dominion over the fish of the sea, and over the fowl of the air, and over the cattle, and over all the earth, and over every creeping thing that creepeth upon the earth.27 So God created man in his own image, in the image of God created he him; male and female created he them. Genesis 1:26-27 KJV

There is nothing more powerful in restoring man back to his original "dominion consciousness" than revisiting God's original intent for creating our species. There is nothing more powerful for effecting total restoration than rediscovering God's original intent. When we examine God's original intent for creating our species we quickly discover that man was created in the image and likeness of God. "Image" implies that man was created of the same exact spiritual substance that God is made of. In other words man's spirit is a chip off God's own Spirit. This means then that man is inherently endued with the same type of creative spirit that is found in God Himself. If such is the case how can men fail to break the tyranny of "TIME and space" over their existence?

The passage also tells us that man was also created in God's likeness. Likeness is a genetic phenomenon. This means that man's DNA is inherently of the God-kind, most especially after we come into the saving knowledge of our Lord Jesus Christ and become the new creation. If we bear God's likeness then we are like God in more ways than most of us dare to believe. When God wanted to dispel the darkness of a formless earth He said, *"Let there be light and there was light!"* God created a new world order by speaking creative faith filled words. Following this same prophetic pattern we can begin to break the "TIME barrier" by speaking creative faith filled words into the atmosphere.

MAN'S DOMINION MANDATE

And God blessed them, and God said unto them, Be fruitful, and multiply, and replenish the earth, and subdue it: and have dominion over the fish of the sea, and over the fowl of the air, and over every living thing that moveth upon the earth. Genesis 1:28 KJV

The above passage of scripture makes it clear that mankind was created to exercise dominion over God's created order here on earth and over the solar system. God told mankind to subdue the earth. Since the solar system, which includes the Sun, the moon, stars and the planetary system, is what controls the entity called "TIME;" man was given power to subdue "TIME." This explains why before the fall of Adam, "TIME" did not exercise any mastery over mankind. Before the fall, Adam was lord of "TIME and space" but this changed drastically after he fell from dominion. But many men and women are about to reverse and overthrow the power of "TIME continuum" over their prophetic destiny.

> *Then God said, "Let lights appear in the sky to separate the day from the night. Let them be signs to mark the seasons, days, and years.* **15** *Let these lights in the sky shine down on the earth." And that is what happened.* **16** *God made two great lights—the larger one to govern the day, and the smaller one to govern the night. He also made the stars.* **17** *God set these lights in the sky to light the earth,* **18** *to govern the day and night, and to separate the light from the darkness. And God saw that it was good.*
>
> Genesis 1:14-18

The above passage of Scripture makes it clear that the Solar system was created on the fourth day of creation. Immediately after God set the Solar system in place He created man and placed him in a place of authority over the rest of His creation. This God given place of supernatural authority spawned the Solar system, animal, plant and maritime kingdoms. This is why once we get restored back to our rightful inheritance in Christ in God; we will begin to break "TIME barriers."

TAKING AUTHORITY OVER TIME

On the day the Lord gave the Israelites victory over the Amorites, Joshua prayed to the Lord in front of all the people of Israel. He said, "Let the sun stand still over Gibeon, and the moon over the valley of Aijalon." **13** *So the sun stood still and the moon stayed in place until the nation of Israel had defeated its enemies. Is this event not recorded in The Book of Jashar? The sun stayed in the middle of the sky, and it did not set as on a normal day. Joshua 10:12-13*

In my humble opinion one of the most powerful biblical demonstration of the power that God gave to mankind to reverse the dictates of "TIME" is the above passage from the book of Joshua. When Joshua and the children

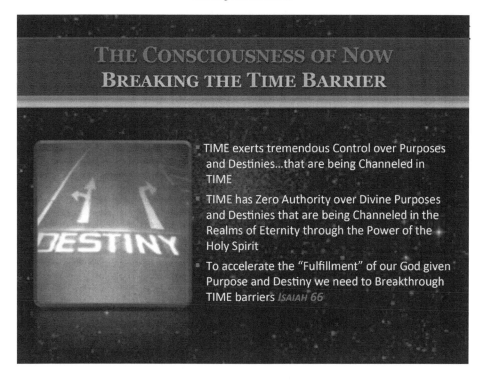

THE CONSCIOUSNESS OF NOW
BREAKING THE TIME BARRIER

- TIME exerts tremendous Control over Purposes and Destinies...that are being Channeled in TIME
- TIME has Zero Authority over Divine Purposes and Destinies that are being Channeled in the Realms of Eternity through the Power of the Holy Spirit
- To accelerate the "Fulfillment" of our God given Purpose and Destiny we need to Breakthrough TIME barriers *ISAIAH 66*

One day the children of Israel were fighting with the Amorites for the rights to the promise land, when Joshua prayed a life altering prayer. Joshua noticed that his forces were prevailing mightily against their enemies. Supernatural grace to prevail over their enemies was upon them. Their enemies were on run but there was only one problem that was threatening their momentum- TIME was running out! The Sun was threatening to set on them before they secured total victory. Joshua quickly came up with a solution to their dilemma. He prayed to God and then commanded the "Sun" to standstill! The bible says that it stood still for twelve hours! Can you imagine 12 hours in which the clock does not move a second forward? Joshua had effectively and supernaturally broken the "TIME Barrier." TIME was no longer a barrier between him and the victory he sought. I truly believe that God is raising men and women who carry the same "Consciousness" over "TIME and space" that Joshua had. These are men and women who know how to live in the "Now!"

BREAKING THE TIME BARRIER THROUGH
THE SPIRIT OF INHERITANCE

You know the saying, 'Four months between planting and harvest.' But I say, wake up and look around. The fields are already ripe for harvest. 36 The harvesters are paid good wages, and the fruit they harvest is people brought to eternal life. What joy awaits both the planter and the harvester alike! 37 You know the saying, 'One plants and another harvests.' And it's true. 38 I sent you to harvest where you didn't plant; others had already done the work, and now you will get to gather the harvest."

John 4:35-38

In closing I want to draw your attention to another master key that the Holy Spirit is going to use in the Last days to help the Body of Christ collapse the "TIME Barrier." This master key is the "spirit of Inheritance." After Adam and Eve fell into Sin, they released a "curse" into the very fabric of their work. This curse manifested itself in the form of "toil and sweat" in everything that they labored to achieve. The only spirit that is powerful enough to overturn and reverse this curse is the spirit of Inheritance. If we work for something its called "wages" but when it is given to us by virtue of a relationship that we have with the person who paid the price its called "Inheritance."

Jesus told his disciples not to say, *"they are yet four months then comes the harvest."* The reason He warned them against this type of thinking is because it subjected them to the dictates of fallen "TIME and space." Jesus did not want His disciples to position themselves inaccurately in how they related to "TIME." He knew that they could not be effective apostles in His Kingdom if they allowed "TIME" to dictate what they could and could not have.

But Yeshua also wanted them to know that there was another spirit in operation that had brought the harvest to them in the "Now" months earlier than they had previously anticipated. He introduces them to this spirit with this expression, *"I sent you to harvest where you didn't plant; others had already done the work, and now you will get to gather the harvest."* How can you harvest where you did not plant? Jesus goes on to tell us how we can reap where we have bestowed no labor- by entering into the work of others. The only thing that can substantiate Yeshua's claim here is the "spirit of Inheritance." Inheritance does not require the "work" of those who are inheriting; it just requires an established relationship between the recipient and the testator. Its only the act of Inheritance that can legally allow us to enjoy another mans work.

While He was on the cross the Lord Jesus Christ cried, "Its finished!" This statement, "its finished" encompasses everything Christ came to do here on earth. It covers the redemption and restoration of everything that Adam and Eve lost in their historic revolt. Jesus went to the cross and paid the full price of our redemption. When we become born again, Jesus becomes our brother. This change in relationship is what qualifies us to enter or reap from other men's labor. If born again believers truly enter into the finished work of Christ we will see a supernatural spirit of acceleration that will change us radically. Its TIME for you to break every "TIME Barrier."

LIFE APPLICATION SECTION

Memory Verse

*Behold, I am with you and will keep you wherever you go, and will bring you back to this land; for I will not leave you until I have done what I have spoken to you." **16** Then Jacob awoke from his sleep and said, "Surely the Lord is in this place, and I did not know it."*

Genesis 28:10-16 (NKJV)

1.   What is the Time Barrier?

2.   What did Joshua do when he saw that time was against him in battle?

Chapter Thirteen

UNLEASHING YOUR CREATIVE JUICES

Since this chapter focuses exclusively on how living in the "Now" will affect the creativity of the Body of Christ worldwide, I want to begin by doing something "out of the box." I will start by referencing a classic folklore story that is widely known – the story of Aladdin and the magic lamp.

"Aladdin is an impoverished young ne'er-do-well in a Chinese town, who is recruited by a sorcerer from the Maghreb, who passes himself off as the brother of Aladdin's late father Qaseem, convincing Aladdin and his mother of his goodwill by apparently making arrangements to set up the lad as a wealthy merchant. The sorcerer's real motive is to persuade young Aladdin to retrieve a wonderful oil lamp from a booby-trapped magic cave of wonder. After the sorcerer attempts to double-cross him, Aladdin finds himself trapped in the cave. Fortunately, Aladdin retains a magic ring lent to him by the sorcerer as protection. When he rubs his hands in despair, he inadvertently rubs the ring, and a jinn, or "genie", appears, who takes him home to his mother. Aladdin is still carrying the lamp, and when his mother tries to clean it, a second, far more powerful genie appears, who is bound to do the bidding of the person holding the lamp.

With the aid of the genie of the lamp, Aladdin becomes rich and powerful and marries Princess Badroulbadour, the Emperor's daughter (after magically foiling her marriage to the vizier's son). The genie builds Aladdin a wonderful palace – a far more magnificent one than that of the Emperor himself.

The sorcerer returns and is able to get his hands on the lamp by tricking Aladdin's wife, who is unaware of the lamp's importance, by offering to exchange "new lamps for old." He orders the genie of the lamp to take the palace along with all its contents to his home in the Maghreb. Fortunately, Aladdin retains the magic ring and is able to summon the lesser genie. Although the genie of the ring cannot directly undo any of the magic of the genie of the lamp, he is able to transport Aladdin to the Maghreb, and help him recover his wife and the lamp and defeat the sorcerer." (http://en.wikipedia.org/wiki/Aladdin)

I chose this story because I want to draw your attention to two thinking processes that distinguish people who are barely getting by, from people who are outrageously successful. These two thinking processes are deductive reasoning and creative thinking. Young Aladdin *inadvertently* awakens a genie that is connected to a magic ring that he was given by the evil sorcerer. Even though this genie was infinitely weaker than the *all mighty genie* that he would also *inadvertently discover inside the magic oil lamp,* he managed through sheer wits and determination to get back to his mother's house using the genie from the ring. The whole time that he is using the aid of the "weaker genie" to find his way home he is holding in his hands an *all mighty genie* that could have taken him to his destination in seconds.

Inadvertently Aladdin and his mother discovered the all-powerful genie in the magic oil lamp. Once he knew how to use this *all-powerful genie,* Aladdin was able to marry the girl of his dreams and amass great fortune. In my humble opinion the weaker genie from Aladdin's magic ring represents the "deductive reasoning" that all men are born with. Deductive reasoning is a thinking process that builds upon information that is already available to us through public domain. By piecing information that is readily available through public domain, most people can achieve a decent level of success.

THE INCREDIBLE POWER OF IMAGINATION

And the Lord came down to see the city and the tower, which the children of men builded.[6]*And the Lord said, Behold, the people is one, and they have all one language; and this they begin to do: and now nothing will be restrained from them,* **which they have imagined to do**

(*Genesis 11:5-6, KJV*).

When young Aladdin discovered the all-mighty genie in his magic oil lamp, his life changed radically at record-speed. I liken Aladdin's all-mighty genie that lived inside the magic oil lamp to man's God-given capacity for imagination. God created people with the ability to exercise their imagination. Unlike deductive reasoning, imagination is more often than not "out-of-the-box thinking." Imagination refuses to be restricted to inventions, technologies, ideas and methods of doing business that are already in the public domain. I liken man's God-given imagination to Aladdin's all-mighty genie. A man's imagination is capable of radically changing his station in life. A person who is willing to use their God-given imagination to come up with life-altering solutions can never stay poor. Great and excessive wealth awaits men and women who have awakened the "genie of their own imagination" in Christ in God.

Before the tower of Babel there were no skyscrapers, no tall buildings like the Eiffel Tower. But man's imagination would soon change history. The Bible tells us that the Godhead came down from heaven to look at what the children of men were building on earth. What is interesting to note here is that even the Lord acknowledged that because the people had one language and one speech whatever they imagined could not be stopped. These men and women had formed a mastermind group in their collective consciousness to build a building tall enough to reach the heavens. The moral of this story is that from antiquity God is showing us the power of man's God-given imagination. Man's imagination is even more powerful when he is submitted to the authority and leading of the Holy Spirit. I believe that one of the most powerful benefits of living in the "Now" is the ability to engage God in our imagination. I believe that God will release His creative ability to the Body of Christ to heal the world's problems, if we would only use our imagination. A wise sage said that the thinking that created today's problems is incapable of fixing them; we, therefore, need a higher level of thinking to help us change course.

WE WERE CUT FROM THE SAME CLOTH

In the beginning God created the heavens and the earth.[2] The earth was formless and empty, and darkness covered the deep waters. And the Spirit of God was hovering over the surface of the waters.[3] Then God said, "Let there be light," and there was light.[4] And God saw that the light was good. Then he separated the light from the darkness.[5] God called the light "day" and the darkness "night"

(Genesis 1:1-5, KJV). [Emphasis added]

The Bible tells us that we are children of the Most High God. If this is true, it means that we were cut out of the same material, so to speak, that God Himself is made of. The Bible is clear that God is one of the most creative beings in the universe. We are introduced to the person of God in the progressive revelation of Scripture just before He begins creating a new world order. We are told in the Genesis account that the earth was without form and void and darkness was on the face of the deep. But when we look at the earth today, it is a mixture of some of the most beautiful rainforests, trees, flowers, animals and birds that will leave you speechless because of their beauty. How did God manage to turn such a mess into a tapestry of breathtaking beauty? He used His infinite imagination to take ashes and turn them into a magnificent work of art.

This is why I am convinced beyond any reasonable doubt that God's people ought to be the most creative people on this planet earth. There is no reason why the Body of Christ should be lagging behind in technology and science in the earth today, when we have access to God's infinite imagination through the power of the Holy Spirit. I believe that the Holy Spirit is changing the consciousness of many members of the Body of Christ and teaching them how to live in the "Now." We will see many creative ideas flood the Body of Christ before the triumphant return of Jesus Christ. For the most part the Church has been reluctant to lead nations in the battle of ideas, but the Holy Spirit is rapidly changing this unfortunate stigma that has maimed the Church's influence on culture.

BECOMING AWARE OF THE PRESENCE OF GOD IN THE NOW!

And Jacob awaked out of his sleep, and he said, Surely the Lord is in this place; and I knew it not

(Genesis 28:16, KJV).

The above Scripture reveals one of the saddest states of the Church today. Jacob sleeps at a place called "Bethel," which literally means the "assembled house of God." While he was sleeping at Bethel, he had a powerful life-changing prophetic dream. In the dream, he sees a ladder that reached up to heaven; and on this ladder there was the ascending and descending of holy angels. At the top of the ladder, Jacob saw the Lord, high and lifted up. In the dream God spoke to Jacob about his prophetic inheritance. God told him that He would transfer the covenantal promises given to Abraham and Isaac to Jacob. When Jacob woke up, he was in a state of shock and awe. He declared, "the *Lord is in this place and I did not know it.*" Unfortunately, this statement is not an isolated case in the Body of Christ; it is a very common experience in the lives of so many of God's people. Many of His children attend church faithfully and they also love Jesus; but many of them have no idea how to experience the presence of God in the "Now." It would seem that the presence of God is always somewhere in the distant future.

Jacob becoming acutely aware of the presence of God in a place that previously seemed mundane, is what I call "consciousness." As we have already stated, "consciousness" is about becoming aware of the daily presence of the living God in our lives in the moment called "Now." It is my humble opinion that a God of the past or a God of the future can never change any human being. The only God who is powerful enough to change human beings has to be the kind of God who is ever relevant and constantly present in the "Now."

In Jacob's later years this prophetic encounter with God that brought him into a place of consciousness, would become his lifeline from living a life of abject poverty in the land of Syria.

When he arrived in Syria Jacob began to work for his uncle Laban. The only problem with working for his uncle Laban is that the man was a crook, who could not be trusted. Laban just about broke every promise he ever gave to his nephew Jacob while he was working for him. Even when it came to marrying his daughters, Laban lied to Jacob on his wedding night. Instead of delivering Rachel to the bedchamber he delivered Leah his eldest daughter. Unfortunately, Leah was not the one Jacob was attracted to. Laban changed Jacob's wages over ten times; so much so that Jacob became very impoverished. Jacob soon realized that if he did not do something, his sleazy uncle would make sure that he was a slave for the rest of his life. Instead of feeling sorry for himself, Jacob reached out to the "God of the Now" who he had met at Bethel. God gave him a very powerful creative idea on how to manipulate the genetics of animals. This is way before the advancement in genetic science that we see today.

PROSPERING THROUGH CREATIVE IDEAS

In this way, God has taken your father's animals and given them to me.[10]*"One time during the mating season, I had a dream and saw that the male goats mating with the females were streaked, speckled, and spotted.*[11]*Then in my dream, the angel of God said to me, 'Jacob!' And I replied, 'Yes, here I am.'*[12]*"The angel said, 'Look up, and you will see that only the streaked, speckled, and spotted males are mating with the females of your flock. For I have seen how Laban has treated you.*[13]*I am the God who appeared to you at Bethel, the place where you anointed the pillar of stone and made your vow to me. Now get ready and leave this country and return to the land of your birth"*

(Genesis 31:9-13).

The world of genetic science continues to get more and more exciting every day, as scientists discover new things about the dynamics of the human genome. Genetic scientists and biochemists are finding the wonders of God that are hidden in the blueprints of man's DNA. But the genetic engineering that the above passage is referencing, happened a long time before the discovery of present day technologies that are enabling scientists to manipulate man's DNA. God told him to place crisscrossed branches of trees in front of animals that were mating in order to reconfigure their genetic template.

At face value, what God told Jacob to do was unthinkable, bordering on foolishness. What He was suggesting Jacob do seemed humanly impossible at the time. It was like asking two black people to mate and give birth to a white baby. Frankly speaking, the chances of a black man and a black woman giving birth to a white baby is genetically impossible. But this is exactly what God was suggesting Jacob do. Jacob received this great idea from heaven. The witty idea that God gave Jacob completely and radically changed his personal economy. Jacob became much richer than Laban; so much so, that Laban's sons began to complain that Jacob had become rich off their father. I believe that God will give the Body of Christ many more creative ideas that will bring the Church into a wealthy place in a single day! He will supernaturally judge the Labans who have stolen from His people in the marketplace. But it will happen through men and women who have a passion to ask Him for creative ideas.

THE KNOWLEDGE OF WITTY INVENTIONS

I wisdom dwell with prudence, and find out knowledge of witty inventions

(Proverbs 8:12, KJV).

When the Body of Christ learns how to live in the moment called "Now" we will see the supernatural release of the knowledge of witty inventions in the Body of Christ. I believe that the Body of Christ should be the global leader in technology, science and medicine. When we start living in the "Now" we will see the release of witty inventions because we are standing in the presence of the wisdom of God. The writer of the book of Proverbs tells us that wisdom brings about the knowledge of witty inventions. The knowledge of witty inventions will change how we do business here in the US and around the world. I believe that the iPhone was given to one of God's children but because many Christians are so religious, God gave it to a Zen Buddhist by the name of Steve Jobs. Fortunately, God is raising a prophetic company of young men and women who are not afraid of functioning in the knowledge of witty inventions for the advancement of the Kingdom of God. These men and women are going to be the pioneers of the future.

THE REVEALER OF SECRETS

*The king answered unto Daniel, and said, Of a truth it is, that your God is a God of gods, and a Lord of kings, and a revealer of **secrets**, seeing thou couldest reveal this secret*

(Daniel 2:47, KJV).

I believe that God is raising an end-time Daniel Company that will change the course of nations. The story of Daniel has fascinated many generations, including minds of Hollywood movie producers. Consequently, many movies about his life have been created. One of the most fascinating aspects of living in the "Now" is found in the book of Daniel. Even the Babylonians knew Daniel as a man who had a very active and dynamic "Now" type of relationship with the Lord. When King Nebuchadnezzar was threatening to kill all the magicians and wise men of Babylon because they could not interpret his dream, Daniel came to the rescue. Daniel made it very clear to King Nebuchadnezzar that the reason he was able to decipher the King's most detailed dream was because he served a God who is a master at revealing secrets. I believe that when the Body of Christ begins to live in the "Now," we are also going to become revealers of secrets. We will be known for solving the most difficult problems of companies, individuals and governments. I believe that living in the "Now" will change the spiritual configuration of the Body of Christ worldwide!

LIFE APPLICATION SECTION

MEMORY VERSE

*And the Lord came down to see the city and the tower, which the children of men builded.*⁶*And the Lord said, Behold, the people is one, and they have all one language; and this they begin to do: and now nothing will be restrained from them,* **which they have imagined to do**

(Genesis 11:5-6, KJV).

1. What is the knowledge of Witty Inventions?

2. Why are God's children supposed to be the most creative people on earth?

Chapter Fourteen

THE PRIESTHOOD OF NOW!

That which hath been is now; and that which is to be hath already been; and God requireth that which is past

(Ecclesiastes 3:15, KJV).

We have already discussed in the previous chapters that the only geometric figure that allows the above passage of Scripture to be true is a circle. We have also stated that in a line, the time measurements past, present and future have their own measure of rule on the consciousness of people who are trapped in this linear world. The only way we can cancel the measure of rule that the past and the future exert on the line is to draw a secular line around point P1, which represents the past and point F1, which represents the future. In the above scenario, the only point that will remain untouched and still exert tremendous influence on the circle is point P2, which represents the present or the moment called "Now." So the questions that come to mind are this; "Is there a priesthood that is compatible with the revelation on the "consciousness of Now"? Is there a priesthood that can operate accurately and comfortably in the moment could "Now"? The answer to these questions is a resounding "Yes"!

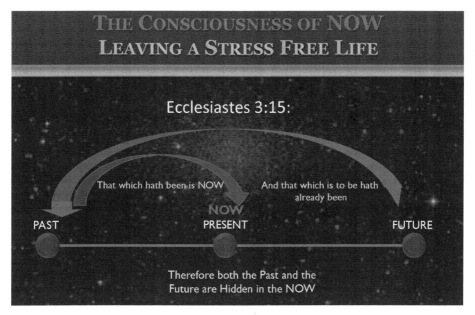

THE MATHEMATICAL PROPERTIES OF A CIRCLE

A priesthood that is compatible with the moment called "Now" must be a priesthood that has the same mathematical properties as a circle. The predominant mathematical property of a circle is that it has no end or beginning. When you look at a circle you cannot pinpoint where it begins and where it ends; in a sense, a circle is everlasting. In the progressive revelation of Scripture God has only revealed two God-ordained priesthoods, the priesthood of Levi and the order of Melchizedek.

> *And here men that die receive tithes; but there he receiveth them, of whom it is witnessed that he liveth.*[9]*And as I may so say, Levi also, who receiveth tithes, payed tithes in Abraham.*[10]*For he was yet in the loins of his father, when Melchisedec met him*
>
> > *(Hebrews 7:8-10, KJV).*

In order to discern which of the two priesthoods God sanctioned to service the spiritual needs of men within the progressive relation of Scripture, we must discern which of the two carry the mathematical properties of the circle. The above passage of Scripture informs us that under the priesthood of Levi, "men who die" received the "tithes" of the people of Israel. The expression "men who die" implies that the priesthood of Levi was a *time sensitive priesthood.* The college of priests who served under the priesthood of Levi was always restricted in their priestly ministry and service by the technology of death. When somebody dies *Time* has run out for such a person. In the above scenario, *Time* exercises lordship on a priesthood that is subject to the technology of death. Anything that is subject to the technology of death is by no means everlasting. This one fact alone completely excludes the priesthood of Levi from being the priesthood that is compatible with the predominant mathematical property of the circle, which is everlasting. A process of elimination leaves us with only one other priesthood to consider in light of the mathematical property that we are looking for.

THE ORDER OF MELCHIZEDEK

> *For this Melchisedec, king of Salem, priest of the most high God, who met Abraham returning from the slaughter of the kings, and blessed him;*[2]*To whom also Abraham gave a tenth part of all; first being by interpretation King of righteousness, and after that also King of Salem, which is, King of peace;*[2]*Without father, without mother, without*

descent, having neither beginning of days, nor end of life; but made like unto the Son of God; abideth a priest continually

(Hebrews 7:1-3, KJV).

The only other priesthood that remains standing is the order of Melchizedek. We will now examine this priesthood in order to determine whether it carries the mathematical properties of the circle. The Bible tells us that Melchizedek was the king of righteousness and king of peace. We are also told that Melchizedek was a priest of the Most High God. The expression "a priest of the Most High God" implies that Melchizedek is such a lofty high priest He has the capacity to stand in the "I AM" Presence of God. Melchizedek's priestly ministry, issues from the very presence of God; he has no intermediary agency between himself and God. But does Melchizedek's priesthood carry the mathematical properties of the circle that we are looking for—everlastingness! If so, then Melchizedek's priesthood is the "Priesthood of the Now."

The writer of the book of Hebrews tells us that the Melchizedek who intercepted Father Abraham in the Valley of kings was no mere mortal. We are told most assuredly that this Melchizedek was *"Without father, without mother, without descent, having neither beginning of days, nor end of life; but made like unto the Son of God; abideth a priest continually."* The expression *"having neither beginning of days, nor end of life"* bestows upon Melchizedek the mathematic property of the circle—everlastingness! Like a circle, He has neither beginning nor end; He administrates His priesthood through the power of an endless life.

A PRIESTHOOD THAT CAN HEAL THE PAST AND SECURE THE FUTURE

The expression *"having neither beginning of days, nor end of life"* also implies definitively that Melchizedek's priesthood can never be defined or restricted by the time measurements of "Past or Future"! *"Having neither beginning of days,"* means that the Melchizedek priesthood can never be relegated to the "Past" as though it carries no immediate power for persons who try to access it at any given moment in time. Since this priesthood transcends the "Past," it is efficacious enough to heal us from any past wounds or trauma. A priesthood that transcends "Time and Space" is capable of reaching back in *Time* to help us make peace with the past.

The expression *"nor end of life"* suggests that Melchizedek's priesthood is also not defined or constrained by the time measurement called "Future"! Furthermore, the expression means that the power of the Melchizedek priesthood of Jesus Christ can never be relegated to sometime in the future as though it is infertile in the moment. This aspect of the Melchizedek priesthood explains why Yeshua refused to allow Martha to postpone His ever-present resurrection power to an imaginary moment in a future time frame when God will raise the dead. Martha declares religiously, "I know that my brother will rise again at the end of time!" To which Jesus replied...

Jesus said unto her, I am the resurrection, and the life: he that believeth in me, though he were dead, yet shall he live

(John 11:25, (KJV).

Martha, in her misinformed religious zeal, almost robs the New Testament of one of its most prolific miracles recorded in Chapter 11 of the book of John – the resurrection of her brother Lazarus. News of Lazarus' terminal illness had reached the ears of Jesus days earlier through an emissary dispatched by Mary and Martha. Instead of rushing to Lazarus' aid, Yeshua stayed four more days. When Jesus finally arrived at the house of Lazarus, he was four days late according to Martha's estimation because her brother had already died days earlier. His dead body in swaddling clothes lay buried inside a tombstone. "Lord, I know that had you been here (notice the past tense here) my brother would never have died!" Martha declared. The implied message in Martha's statement is, "Lord, I don't believe that You can heal my dead brother now, but had You been here while he was sick, You would have healed him." Martha's response is typical of the Body of Christ today. We believe that God's power only worked for past generations of super saints. There are those among us who believe passionately that God's supernatural power will be made readily available to us in a future "Time frame." The only problem with this way of thinking is that God's power is always available to us in the "Now." God will not be any more powerful tomorrow than He is today. Martha did not realize that Yeshua was the manifestation of the Melchizedek priesthood in bodily form; a priesthood that functions perpetually in the "Now" beyond the restrictions of time and space. This is why the Melchizedek priesthood is the only priesthood that can truly heal the past and secure the future most humans find so elusive.

KING OF RIGHTEOUSNESS AND PEACE

For this Melchisedec, king of Salem, priest of the most high God, who met Abraham returning from the slaughter of the kings, and blessed him; ²To whom also Abraham gave a tenth part of all; first being by interpretation King of righteousness, and after that also King of Salem, which is, King of peace

(Hebrews 7:1-2, KJV).

126

The writer of the book of Hebrews boldly declares that this Melchizedek who intercepted Abraham was "King of righteousness and peace." Righteousness is the condition of being in right standing or alignment with a governing authority. There is no governing authority that is higher or more consequential than the Most High God. If any human is not in a place of righteousness (right standing with Him) they will struggle to retain mastery over the dictates of "Time continuum" on their consciousness. The Scripture declares "There is no peace for the wicked" (Isaiah 48:22).

What is Peace? Peace suggests a tranquility of spirit, mind and emotions that is beyond the reach of the engines of chaos that are common to all. "Peace" in Hebrew Orthodoxy carries the meaning of being delivered from the principle that binds a person to chaos. The Hebrew word for "Peace" is "Shalom," which means "nothing missing, nothing broken or out of place." It is easy to see why "Peace" is one of the greatest weapons against the tyranny of stress. Peace and stress cannot live in the same space at the same time. They are mutually exclusive spiritual technologies. The major difference between these two forces is that stress causes our bodies to vibrate at a much lower frequency than most diseases. This makes us susceptible to all kinds of ailments. Peace on the other hand vibrates at a very high frequency as it issues directly from the throne of God. But without righteousness, there can be no peace. The Melchizedek priesthood is an everlasting priesthood God has made available to the sons of men that can align us with Him in the "Now," while infusing us with peace that surpasses all human comprehension.

LIFE APPLICATION SECTION

Memory Verse

For this Melchisedec, king of Salem, priest of the most high God, who met Abraham returning from the slaughter of the kings, and blessed him;² To whom also Abraham gave a tenth part of all; first being by interpretation King of righteousness, and after that also King of Salem, which is, King of peace;² Without father, without mother, without descent, having neither beginning of days, nor end of life; but made like unto the Son of God; abideth a priest continually

(Hebrews 7:1-3, KJV*)*.

1. What is the mathematical property of a circle that lends itself to eternity?

2. Why is the Melchizedek priesthood a priesthood of the "Now"?

REFERENCES

(Article from www.stopfollowingman.org)   Preface

(Article from www.ministeringdeliverance.com) page 67

Article by Apostle Jonas Clark: http://www.jonasclark.com/spiritual-warfare-prayer/sex-soul-ties-jezebel-seducing-spirit.html#ixzz2nOu3czce

Copyrights (c) Jonas Clark Ministries

http://en.wikipedia.org/wiki/Aladdin   page 93

Made in the USA
San Bernardino, CA
13 February 2014